W9-ATJ-424

Acknowledgments

It's important to me that I publicly thank all the people who have helped with the preparation and writing of this book: Jack Frakes, my own high school drama teacher, who not only inspired me all those years ago, but read early versions of this work and made helpful suggestions; my father, Thomas L. Lee, president of my fan club and ace proofreader — and my mother, Irene, the vice president and head cheerleader; my brother, Lawrence W. Lee, who got me started with computers and encouraged me at every opportunity; Berenda Crellin, who taught me more about acting, and about myself, than all the other acting teachers I ever had; my students over the years, who have taught me a great deal; Ed Arriaga and Suzanne Ashby, successive principals of Rincon High School, who found money in the lean budget for printing copies of this book for use in my own classes; my wife, Maggie, and my family, who tolerated me during all those hours at the keyboard, and who still love me (I believe) in spite of all the time and energy I spent working at home.

EVERYTHING ABOUT
THEATRE!

The guidebook of
theatre fundamentals

ROBERT L. LEE

MERIWETHER PUBLISHING LTD.
Colorado Springs, Colorado

Meriwether Publishing Ltd., Publisher
P.O. Box 7710
Colorado Springs, CO 80933

Editor: Theodore O. Zapel
Typesetting: Sharon E. Garlock
Cover design: Tom Myers

Library of Congress Cataloging-in-Publication Data

Lee, Robert L. (Robert LeRoy), 1945-
    Everything about theatre! : a comprehensive survey about the arts
and crafts of the stage / by Robert L. Lee. -- 1st ed.
        p.   cm.
    ISBN 1-56608-019-3 (pbk.)
    1. Theater--Production and direction. 2. Acting. 3. Theater--
History.   I. Title.
PN2053.L395   1996
792--dc20   96-6742
                                                          CIP
                                                          AC

2   3   4   5   6   7   8   99 98 97

CONTENTS

INTRODUCTION

If it's true that "All the world's a stage, and all the men and women merely players," then why should anyone bother to study drama or theatre? Well, because it's just not as simple as all that!

Shakespeare was talking about the way all of us play different "roles" during our lives: the infant, the child, the youth, the adult, and so on. A few moments' reflection on our daily lives reveals that we also play more than one part at the same age. We often change "characters" when we change our surroundings, playing one role at home but quite a different one at school, or at a party, or at work.

But the business of theatre is different. It's different because of the nature of our *intent*. Playing varied roles in life is usually effortless, easy, natural. Doing the same thing on purpose, on a stage in front of strangers, is effortful, difficult, and even unnatural.

And that's only the tip of the theatrical iceberg. It may be true that the minimum requirements for theatre are an actor and an audience, but most of us expect that there will also be a well-written script, scenery, costumes, lighting, properties, sound effects. And we accept as necessary those collateral activities such as preparing and distributing programs, advertising and selling tickets, and providing comfortable seating, clean restrooms, and accessible parking!

The involvement of all these people (designers, writers, actors, directors, producers, carpenters, painters, seamstresses, stagehands, lighting and sound technicians, just to name a few) has led to the description of theatre as a collaborative art. Each member of the collaboration must bring several things to the job at hand, if the play is to have a chance at success.

Each person must have a certain level of expertise in his or her own field. A lighting designer or technician, for example, is expected to know quite a lot about electricity (burning down the theatre is not a good idea), physics (how colored light reacts with other colors in lights as well as in the costumes, scenery, and makeup), available lighting instruments (which type to use to produce the desired effect of light and shadow), and æsthetics and timing to be able to assist the director and cast in producing the desired effect on the audience during the performance.

Similar levels of knowledge are required from each member of the collaborative team. But that's not the end of the story. Each person must bring good work habits to the task (Actors' Equity rules call for an actor to be fired if he is "tardy" to rehearsal more than once!). The ability to work with others is essential. And each person must have a love of theatre, a willingness to sacrifice time, energy, and even his own ego for the good of the production as a whole.

The purpose of a high school drama or theatre arts program is to introduce you to as many aspects of drama as possible, to allow you to experience for yourself the diversity and excitement of theatre, and to encourage you to develop the love of theatre which is necessary for the successful production of a play at any level: high school, college, community theatre, or professional. It's not realistic to expect that you will enjoy each area of study equally, nor that you will be equally good at each area. It *is* realistic to expect that you will keep an open mind, doing the best you can with each assignment.

Those who successfully complete one or more courses based on the material in this book will have learned enough to be more discriminating consumers of theatre. They may have discovered an outlet for their creative energies which will last a lifetime, even if they don't pursue theatre as a profession. And they will have acquired skills which will be useful in almost any future endeavor.

This book is not designed to provide professional training. It is neither an acting book, nor a stagecraft book, nor a book in any of the specific areas of theatre. I hope that you will learn enough about theatre to want to continue your studies, becoming expert in one or more areas. More than that, I hope you discover some things about the world, life in general, and about yourself.

Robert L. Lee

Tucson, Arizona
Summer, 1994

CHAPTER ONE

LEARNING YOUR WAY AROUND

Most people recognize that learning your way around is one of the most important goals for a newcomer to any environment. A theatre is no exception. As the year goes along, it will be important for you to be able to find your way around our theatre, and many of the places here have names that are the same in other theatres around the world.

"Tell the cast not to walk through the house when they come to the stage from the green room," the director says to the stage manager. But what on earth did he mean?

Welcome to the Theatre!

The stage, of course, is the part of the theatre where the acting takes place during a performance, and most people know that. Fewer know that the part of the theatre where the audience sits is called the house, or that the room where the actors wait for their entrance cues is called, by long tradition and regardless of the color of the walls or floor, the green room. The green room is usually located near the stage and convenient to the dressing rooms.

Most theatres also have a box office, and many school theatres have a small library, too.

And what's the difference between an auditorium and a theatre? If you think about the word *audio*, it will come as no surprise that an auditorium was originally a place for hearing something. It's less obvious that the Greek word *theatron* originally meant a seeing place.

1

Any working theatre has space set aside for the construction and painting of scenery and props. Unless the theatre is large enough to have separate facilities for each of these activities, they are combined in one room called, simply, the shop.

Some older theatres use a space just off-stage for their lighting control system, but newer theatres have a control booth (or sometimes separate light and sound booths) located at the back of the house so that the technicians can see the performance from the point of view of the audience.

Storage space is usually at a premium in a theatre. Space is needed for small props such as plates, cups and saucers, cookware, glasses, vases, etc. Furniture pieces, luggage, platforms, and scenery pieces need storage space, too, as well as costumes and fabric pieces such as curtains and tablecloths. Then there are things like makeup supplies, lighting equipment, lumber, paint, tools...well, you get the idea. There is almost never as much room as there is stuff to put in it!

Theatre Designs

It's worth taking some time to learn about different types of theatres. The proscenium theatre is still the most common type, and many of the terms used there have been adapted for use in other theatres.

The most important feature of this traditional theatre is that it is essentially two separate buildings, a horizontal one that contains the house, and a vertical one that contains the stage. The two buildings are connected by an opening through which the audience views the stage. This opening is called a proscenium arch. Proscenium means, literally, in front of the scene.

Because the audience looks at the stage through this "hole in the wall," this theatre is sometimes said to have a "picture frame" stage. The separateness of the two areas reduces the feeling of intimacy that's possible in a theatre that's "all in one room," especially if there is an orchestra pit between the stage and the front row of seats. Nevertheless, many people today find that they are more comfortable in a proscenium theatre, perhaps because it closely resembles a movie theatre or even a TV screen.

Proscenium theatres offer many advantages to the scenic designer. Because so much of the stage house is invisible to the audience, it's easy to shift and store several different settings for a single play. Flat scenery (curtains, drops, framed drops, legs, portals, etc.) and certain other pieces (chandeliers, for example) can be "flown" into the upper reaches of the *scene house* in just a few seconds. Depending on the size of the space off-stage left and right (commonly called the *wings*), three-dimensional scenery such as wagons, platforms, even entire sets, can be moved off-stage under the cover of the closed curtain.

A well-designed and well-equipped proscenium theatre also benefits the lighting designer, especially in traditional productions. All of the spotlights, floodlights, and strip lights used in a production can be hidden from view up in the *flies*, in the wings, or in various locations in the house, such as a *beam port* cut through the ceiling above the audience. The audience sees only the results of the designer's work as the light illuminates the actors and scenery, without having their attention drawn to the sources of that light.

At one time or other, theatre people have used almost every conceivable arrangement of performing and viewing spaces. Some of them are shown in the drawings here and on the next page. Become familiar with as many different theatre types as possible. Find opportunities to visit other theatres. Explore the differences in audience–cast relationship, the way the theatre itself determines play selection and scenic styles, and how technical aspects of the show, such as lighting and shifting, are handled.

Then, the next time you go with your family or friends to see a show or concert, your easy familiarity with things theatrical will astound them as you discuss the type of theatre (or other performance space) you're in and the relative advantages and disadvantages of different styles of theatres and auditoriums!

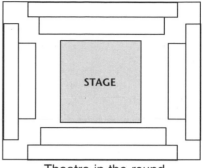

Theatre-in-the-round

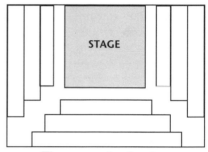

Three-quarter theatre

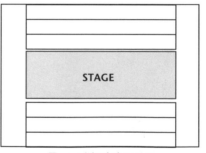

Two-sided theatre

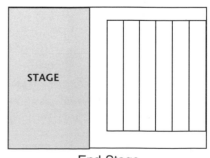

End Stage

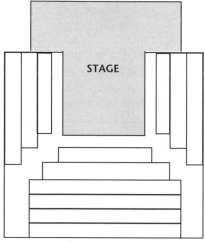

Thrust Stage

Exercises:

1. Tour your theatre or performing space. Then, with a partner, draw a floor plan or diagram of the theatre. Make the rooms proportional to each other, but don't worry about accurate scale. Be sure to include all storage and work areas, and the location of exits and fire extinguishers.

2. Tour a proscenium theatre — if your theatre isn't one! Be sure you see (and remember) each of the following: proscenium, ante-pro, beam port, wings, apron, orchestra pit, pin rail, loading rail, arbor, batten, stage weight, grid, fly space, legs, border, teaser, tormentor, and drop.

3. Write a two-page report in which you discuss the advantages and disadvantages of proscenium theatres and another type (theatre-in-the-round, thrust stage, etc.) as performing spaces.

CHAPTER TWO
INTRODUCTION TO ACTING

For most students, acting is the most interesting (perhaps the only interesting) part of a drama course. Acting is certainly the most visible part of the theatrical (or television or motion picture) product, and our society spends a great deal of time, energy, and money satisfying its curiosity about those actors who are called stars.

Experienced actors and theatre teachers find that there is an unfortunate side effect of the flood of television shows, theatrical films, and most recently, video rentals. There is so much "product" available, and so much of it is reasonably well produced, that a vast majority of us have the opinion that acting is easy. After all, look at all the ex-football players, wrestlers, and weight lifters who have become famous in the movies and on television!

The trouble is that most people confuse being a celebrity with being an actor. Hollywood, of course, does its best to keep this confusion strong because celebrities sell tickets — whether or not they can act. This confusion not only reduces our critical skills, making it difficult for us to evaluate the worth of a particular performance, it leads too many people to the conclusion that knowledge, skills, training, and rehearsal are not necessary, that they are, in fact, a waste of time.

Nobody starts taking music lessons by demanding an immediate concert date.

There is an old joke about a young man carrying a violin case who stops an elderly man on a New York City street corner.

"How do I get to Carnegie Hall?" the young man asks.

"Practice, my boy, practice!" responds the older gentleman.

No one, not even the presumably talented and well-trained young man in the joke, would expect to begin taking music lessons by preparing for an immediate concert performance. It is accepted that practice — scales and fingering exercises — is as important to a future musician as weight training, wind sprints, and repetitive drills are important to a future athlete.

But, things being what they are, the situation is different with acting. Your introduction to acting will be as gentle and gradual as possible. Keep in mind, however, that acting is not easy. And good acting is extremely difficult.

Stage Geography

Imagine that you have been rehearsing a play for several days when you receive the following message:

TO: Cast members

FROM: Director

SUBJECT: Blocking

Here is the corrected blocking for first half of p. 47, II, 2. Please write in your script and execute at next rehearsal.

SUSAN: on first line, XDL to above sofa.

MARK: From your position at LC, CXDR2, stand ¼ R

TED: X to DRC below chair. Move chair 2 feet off.

SUSAN: X below sofa, sit at on-stage end.

TED: X in 2, stand ¾ L

Now what? What is that all about? Do you need Captain Astro's Secret Decoder Ring to figure it out? Not if you read the explanation!

Stage directions in proscenium theatres are given in terms of up, down, right, and left. *Up* is away from the audience, and *down* is towards the audience. *Left* and *right* are *always* used from the point of view of the actor facing the audience. It's a good idea to get used to thinking of the stage as if it were marked off with painted lines into nine separate areas, identified as they are in the diagram at left on the next page. The diagram at right shows an additional six areas that are commonly used. The areas are almost always abbreviated: DL for down left, UC for up center, DRC for down right center, and so on.

X MARKS THE SPOT?

Actors and directors use X as an abbreviation for the word CROSS, meaning *move across the stage*, as in *X to door* (cross to the door). A counter-cross (CX) is a movement designed to help balance the stage and keep one actor from upstaging another. It is a short cross in the direction opposite (counter) to the one just taken by another actor.

STAGE	Up Right	Up Center	Up Left
	Right	Center	Left
	Down Right	Down Center	Down Left

STAGE	Up Right	Up Center	Up Left
		URC	ULC
	Right	RC Center LC	Left
		DRC	DLC
	Down Right	Down Center	Down Left

HOUSE

Besides being the name of an area, each term is also used to indicate a direction of movement. An actor standing at UC may be directed to XDL2 (cross DL 2 steps). That doesn't mean he is expected to move all the way to the DL area in two giant steps. It means, "Take two steps in the direction of DL."

What about that strange direction, *X below sofa*? Will Mary have to make herself very small and slither under the furniture? Fortunately not! The directions *below* (and *above*) mean on the downstage (upstage) side of the sofa, or other piece of furniture or person.

And how about the *on-stage end of sofa*? Is one end of the sofa hidden from the audience? Actually, on and off are terms used to indicate movement or location toward or away from an imaginary line drawn from down center to up center. The on-stage end of the sofa is the end closer to center stage.

When an actor is directed to *X in 2*, it usually means she or he should take two steps (or at any rate move a short distance) toward another actor. It's the opposite of away.

Body Positions

Which way an actor faces is important. In life outside the theatre, two people holding a conversation are likely to stand facing each other. On stage, though, two actors rarely face each other. Instead they *open up*, each one turning just a little toward downstage. This allows the audience to get a better look at both actors' faces.

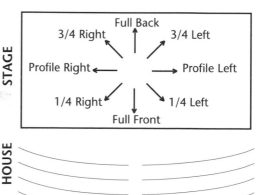

There are eight basic body positions — or directions to face — for actors. Remember that the Left and Right designations refer to the side of the stage the actor is facing, not to the side of his face we can see.

Other Useful Terms

Here's a short (yes, short) list of other words and phrases that will be handy for you to know. Read through the list, then use it for reference.

Ad-lib: Make up words or actions, usually to cover a mistake in a performance.

Anticipating: Reacting to something before your character has any reason to. Although you (the actor) know perfectly well that somebody is coming up behind you, your character, who is supposedly experiencing all this for the very first time, has no way of knowing until the other character makes a noise or says a line or walks where you can see him or her.

At Rise: The moment when the curtain rises, or the stage lights go on, or whatever happens to signal the start of the play or act or scene.

Black-out: The end of an act or play, or the time between scenes of an act during which the stage lights are off and/or the curtain is closed.

Blocking: The movement of the characters (actors) on the stage.

Breaking character: Becoming yourself on the stage, instead of the character you're playing. Audiences can always tell when an actor breaks character. It's one of the cardinal sins for an actor. Making eye contact with the audience, giggling or laughing, muttering words to yourself or the audience or other actors — these are some of the signs of breaking character.

Compass directions: Some theatres, particularly those with audience seating on all sides of the stage, use North, South, East, and West instead of the traditional Up, Down, Left, and Right. Another variation is the "clock" system, assigning the twelve numbers of the clock face to the stage.

Cue: The line spoken just before your line, or the signal for you to enter or perform another action.

Discovered: Already on the stage when the scene begins.

Down-stage turn: Turning so that your body passes through the full front position on your way to your final position.

Gesture: Generally, any action performed with the hands and arms, or the head (as in a nod).

Going up: Forgetting your lines on-stage.

Holding for a laugh: Allowing the audience's response to *begin* dying away before continuing. You need to top the remaining laughter, rather than let it die away completely.

Indicating: *Telling* the audience something instead of *showing* them; using clichés or tired generalizations in your acting instead of honest and revealing actions and emotions.

Intention: What your character wants in a scene, best expressed in a vivid sentence with a strong verb. *I want to kick him down the stairs*, for example, even in a scene where your character couldn't possibly engage in a physical attack.

Interior monolog: The entire stream of thoughts that a character thinks while he or she is on stage, speaking or listening, moving or still.

Motivation: The *character's* reason for doing or saying a particular thing. The director may tell you to cross to the fireplace because he needs you out of the way before the star's big entrance, but it's up to you to figure out a reason for the character to move (since the character has never even heard of the director).

Objective: What a character wants in a scene. See **Intention**.

Observation: Studying other people as sources for your character's voice and movement. For example, watching the way older people walk and listening to the way they talk when preparing to play an older character.

Projecting: Making sure your performance is audible and visible from every seat in the house.

Picking up cues: Reducing the amount of time between speeches, usually accomplished by inhaling during the preceding speech (rather than after it) so that you are prepared to speak immediately. Cues can also be picked up physically, by a gesture or movement — something that shows the audience where to look and assures them that nobody has gone up in his lines.

Pointing a line: Drawing attention to a particular speech — or part of a speech — by vocal or physical means. For example, one item in a list can be pointed by a short pause before it, or by stopping a repetitive movement (such as knitting, or pacing) just before saying the word.

Reason and Thought: An intellectual approach to discovering appropriate movements and vocal traits. If your character is a retired professional football player, for example, his accumulated injuries might very well make him walk and move a little stiffly — like a person with arthritis.

Stage business: Activities performed on stage as a part of your characterization. Sometimes they are directly related to the action of the play (as *tearing up the incriminating letter*). Sometimes they are not directly related to the action of the play (as *sweeping the floor during a breakfast scene*). Business like this is sometimes called an *independent activity*. In either case, the business must reveal something about your character to the audience.

Subtext: The thoughts that underlie the character's actual words (the text). The subtext often determines the specific way a line is said. For example, the exact meaning and delivery of the line, "What time is it?" will vary according to the sub-text. A condemned prisoner awaiting execution will be thinking, "How much longer do I have to live?" while a person attending a boring lecture might be thinking, "When will this be over?"

Top or Topping: Delivering your line so that it is stronger than the one just before it.

Upstaging: Causing another actor to have to turn into a closed position so that the audience can't see his face, usually accomplished by moving upstage so that when the other person turns to face you he is in a ¾ position.

Exercise:

With a partner, prepare the Basic Stage Movement exercise, as shown in Appendix B, page 195.

CHAPTER THREE

THEATRE'S FAMILY ALBUM: ANCIENT THEATRE

Just when you thought it was safe to go to drama class, you discover that it's not going to be simply acting after all! But why, you may ask, should we bother to study theatre history? Who cares, anyway, what those guys did a long time ago? How is knowing about all that old stuff going to help me today or tomorrow or next year?

I'm glad you asked! Now let me ask you a question: do you own a camera or wish you did? Why? (I know, I know that's two questions, but at least they're related.) The fact is that people like to take snapshots of their friends, their families, places they live, and places they visit. More important is the fact that people enjoy looking at the photos later. Many of you have access to an album or box of old family pic-

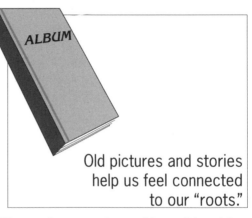

Old pictures and stories help us feel connected to our "roots."

tures, and at some time in your life you have sat down (if possible with a parent or grandparent) to look through the pictures.

It's fun to see how we looked when we were younger, and how our parents looked when they were children, and how people dressed when Grandpa was a boy. The hair styles are a scream, and isn't it funny that they were so proud of that old car? And look at this picture of Mom's Aunt Edna! That's where I got my nose and eyes!

We find out a great deal about ourselves when we look at old pictures. Where we came from, who we came from, how we got to be the way we are. Looking at old pictures, and listening to stories that begin, "I remember when...," help us establish a connection with our family, a feeling that although we are unique individuals, we are also part of a unique group.

What we are going to do is the equivalent of looking through the Theatre Family Album. Of course, there aren't photographs of the ancient (or even the very old!) theatres and actors, and not even your teacher is old enough to truthfully say, "I remember when Shakespeare was all the rage on the London social scene," but we'll do the best we can — because it's important for us as individual members of the theatre family to find out where we came from, who we came from, and how we got to be the way we are.

The Earliest Theatre

For as long as there have been historians, there has been speculation about the origins of theatre. A commonly held opinion is that early man engaged in camp-fire enactments of scenes from the hunt, for example, perhaps even before the development of language. These scenes, no doubt crudely acted by our standards, possibly served in the beginning as simply a way to show "what happened today (or yesterday, or last year) in the big hunt when Oog fell down and the giant bear ate him."

It seems clearer that later on, these scenes took on a ritualistic nature, becoming a part of the religion of the people. There would probably have been music, dancing, and chanting, as well as rudimentary costumes, makeup, or masks. The acting out of a successful hunt was possibly expected to bring about success in tomorrow's hunt.

Notice, please, all the qualifiers in the two preceding paragraphs — *opinion, possibly, perhaps, probably.* These are necessary because nobody knows for sure what happened so long ago. We can examine the records we do have, and investigate primitive peoples and cultures still to be found in certain areas of today's world, but in the end, we can only make informed guesses about the very earliest expressions of mankind's theatrical flair.

While there is evidence of dramatic performances at Knossos, on the island of Crete in the Mediterranean Sea, it is from ancient Egypt that we find our first evidence of regular presentation of religious and civic drama. Plays were performed to honor the pharaoh at his coronation, to assist in curing the sick, and to celebrate Egyptian religious beliefs. No actual scripts have survived the five thousand years or so since the earliest Egyptian plays. Our evidence comes mostly from wall paintings and other artifacts. Most is known about the Abydos Passion Play, which tells the story of the battle between the gods Set and Osiris, ending when Isis (Osiris' wife) steals Osiris' dismembered body from Set and buries it, thus creating the fertile ground of Egypt and making Osiris the lord of the underworld.

Greek Theatre

It was across the Mediterranean Sea from Egypt that drama reached such a peak of importance and excellence that a fairly substantial record has survived. For the first time our family album contains actual names of playwrights and actors, and there are scripts that have survived.

The flowering of Greek drama had its roots in Greek religion. Primitive celebrations in honor of the god of wine and fertility, Dionysus, included a group of chanting dancers around an altar. The *dithyramb* they chanted evolved into Greek tragedy, and the dancers became known as the chorus.

Tragedy, literally translated as *goat song*, became a focal point of the City Dionysia, held in Athens each spring. The festival ended with a competition between playwrights. Each competitor presented a tragic *trilogy* (three plays on the same theme) and one *satyr play* in which the same theme was treated comically. The winning playwright, and the *choregos*, or city-appointed producer, were awarded the coveted laurel wreath.

By the fifth century B.C., called the Golden Age of Greece, a man named *Thespis of Attica* had "invented" acting by designating one member of the chorus to stand apart from the others and respond to them. (That's why actors are still called Thespians.) The theatre itself had evolved from a cleared space at the foot of a hill into a grand, open-air *amphitheater.*

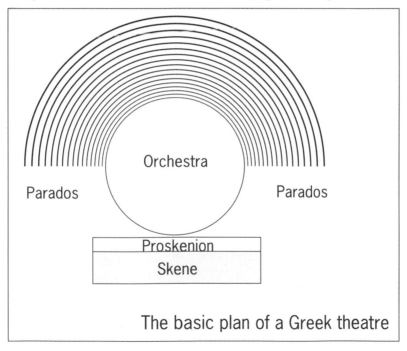

Orchestra

Parados

Parados

Proskenion

Skene

The basic plan of a Greek theatre

The theatre was carved from a hillside, providing bench-style seating for very large crowds. The chorus entered the *orchestra*, or dancing place, via one of the *paradoi*. Actors changed costumes in a building called the *skene*, in front of which was added a raised platform called the *proskenion* (remember "proscenium"?).

The Staging of Greek Drama

In each period in history, theatrical practice has developed a set of special ways of doing things. These special practices are called *conventions,* and those in use during a particular period are determined by the traditions and circumstances surrounding the theatre at that particular time. Let's take a look at some of the conventions of Greek theatre.

Because the dramas evolved from choral dances and chants, the *chorus* remained a strong presence in Greek tragedy throughout the Golden Age and beyond. The addition of one actor, by Thespis, was a major step forward, and was later followed by the addition of two more actors. This means that in most plays from the period, only *three actors* played all the major roles.

How did three people play all those parts? Quick changes of costume and makeup? Well, sort of! Because the plays were performed in such large, outdoor theatres, actors may have worn elevated shoes, tall headpieces, and large *masks.* All these helped the actors to be seen in the back rows, and the mask might have functioned as a miniature megaphone, helping to project the actor's voice. In addition, the use of masks made it relatively simple for one actor to play several parts!

Two sides of
a *periaktos*

The need to be seen and heard by such large crowds also had an effect on the style of playwriting and acting. Plays and performances were much more declamatory than we are used to. Long speeches are the rule, rather than quick exchanges of dialog. And the speeches were probably delivered more to the audience than to the other characters, taking away even more of the realism we usually expect today.

Scenery was slow to develop and remained fairly limited. The *skene* could be used to represent several different locales by placing painted panels between or in front of the columns of its facade or front wall. Quicker shifts of scene could be accomplished through the use of *periaktoi,* triangular prisms which could be pivoted to reveal three different backgrounds.

The use of another piece of scenery, the *eccyclema,* was dictated by the convention that all *violence must take place off-stage,* out of sight of the audience. Usually a messenger or other character would enter and tell about the murder, or suicide, or whatever. Sometimes the telling would be accompanied by the wheeling in of the *eccyclema*, a wheeled platform we'd call a wagon today, containing the mangled and bloody bodies.

One other scenic device played an important part in many Greek plays. This was a crane-like machine by which an actor playing the part of a god and riding in a large basket could be lowered onto the stage from above. This *deus ex machina* (god from the machine) was used as a device to conveniently assist the human characters in solving their problems by divine intervention, and the phrase is still used to indicate a fortuitous event or coincidence which happens at just the right time to save someone (in a play or in life) from disaster.

The Greek Playwrights

Much of what we know about Greek theatre comes from the few surviving scripts of three great writers of tragedy and one comic playwright. Their names, the titles of some of their plays, and some specific information about a few of the plays are important entries in our album.

Æschylus

Æschylus (525-456 B.C.) is often called the Father of Tragedy. His plays dealt with the interaction between gods and men, with emphasis on the inevitability of suffering. His *Oresteia* trilogy tells the story of the House of Atreus, and illustrates two important religious beliefs of the Greeks.

In *Agamemnon*, the first play of the trilogy, Agamemnon returns from ten years of fighting a war. He acts with *hubris*, a sinful excess of pride, and is killed by his wife, Clytemnestra, who has never forgiven him for sacrificing their eldest daughter to the gods before the war.

This murder triggers the vengeance theme in the next two parts of the trilogy. It was a religious obligation of the Greeks to avenge a wrong done to one's family, and in *The Libation Bearers*, Electra — the remaining daughter of Agamemnon — talks her brother, Orestes, into killing their mother.

The final play of the trilogy, *The Furies*, finds Orestes being chased and hounded throughout the world by the supernatural Furies. His sin, of course, is that of matricide, and it seems to require an act of vengeance in return. At the last minute Orestes is pardoned by the gods.

Sophocles

The second great writer of tragedies was Sophocles (497-406 B.C.), who was also responsible for the addition of the third actor to the stage. Although we know he wrote over one hundred plays, winning the City Dionysia prize eighteen times, only seven of his plays have survived. These include *Electra*, his version of the Oresteia theme, and his great Œdipus trilogy.

Œdipus Rex (Œdipus the King) tells the story of how Œdipus saves the city of Thebes at the cost of discovering that he has murdered his father and married his own mother in an effort to avoid exactly that fate. His mother-wife kills herself, and Œdipus puts his own eyes out and condemns himself to exile and a life as a blind beggar. The rest of his life — and his death — is the story of the second play, *Œdipus at Colonnus*.

The trilogy ends with Antigone, in which Œdipus' younger daughter, Antigone, sacrifices her life in a futile attempt to fulfill another important religious obligation. When her two broth-

> **Aeschylus wrote about gods, Sophocles wrote about heroes, and Euripedes wrote about men.**

ers kill each other in a battle to determine which one will rule the city, their uncle, Creon, decrees that one body be brought into the city and buried with honors while the other is left to rot in the fields. Antigone fails to talk her sister, Ismene, into helping her, and tries twice to complete the ritual burial of her brother. When she is caught for the second time, Creon feels he has no choice but to have her killed, a decision which costs him the lives of his wife and only son.

Euripedes

Euripedes (480?-405 B.C.) was the youngest, most modern and least popular of the three great writers of tragedy. His plays differed from those of his contemporaries in their emphasis on psychological motivation and social consciousness. He also appealed to the emotions by including in his plays a look at the small details of the daily lives of his characters.

His *Medea* tells of the mythological sorceress who helped Jason win the Golden Fleece. After their marriage she continues to assist Jason in his rise to power, but he abandons her for Glauce, a daughter of Creon. Driven mad by jealousy, Medea takes her revenge on Jason by gruesomely murdering their two children.

The Trojan Women is one of the most powerful antiwar plays ever written. After the defeat of Hector, of the House of Priam, at Troy, the Greek generals sacrifice one of Hector's daughters and throw his son from the battlements to ensure the end of the royal line. Then Helen, Hector's other daughter and the object of the whole war, arrives and is able to woo Menelaus into sparing her life. The Greek generals are shown as weak, cruel cowards, reflecting Euripedes' disgust over the slaughter by the Athenians of the inhabitants of the island of Melos for their neutrality in the recent war with Sparta.

Euripedes' social conscience is also evident in his other plays. *Alcestis* attacks the commonly held opinion that women are subservient to men, and *Hippolytus* attacks the unjust treatment of illegitimate children.

Aristophanes

Eleven surviving plays of Aristophanes (445-c.380 B.C.) are the only examples we have of what is called Old Comedy. Aristophanes wrote very funny, and therefore very popular, social satire. He poked fun at public figures such as Socrates (*The Clouds*), and Euripedes (*The Frogs*). His attacks extended to modern trends in music and philosophy, and he was not above having the gods come out second best.

His comic genius has been dimmed over the centuries because it was so closely tied to what were then the current events of the day. One play, *Lysistrata*, demonstrates his ability, along with the bawdiness of Old Comedy, and is still performed today.

In *Lysistrata*, the title character decides to put an end to the twenty-one-year-old Peloponnesian war. She calls the other wives to a secret meeting outside the city and recruits them to her cause. They agree to shut themselves away from their husbands until the war is concluded, and in the end, Lysistrata has the satisfaction of dictating the terms of surrender.

Menander

As you might suspect, where there was an Old Comedy, there was a New Comedy. The only surviving work of this style was written by Menander (c.342-292 B.C.). Until *The Curmudgeon* was discovered in the late 1950s, only fragments of his plays had been found, and most of what we knew of his works was learned from studying the Roman playwrights who copied him.

Menander wrote comedies dealing with daily life and domestic situations. His plays featured characters such as clever servants, protective fathers, and young lovers — types who have been standards in the comic theatre ever since.

Exercises:

Select one of the following projects.

1. Read one of the following plays and write a report on it. Present your report orally to the class.

   > *Agamemnon, The Libation Bearers, The Furies, or Prometheus Bound,* by Æschylus.
   >
   > *Electra, Œdipus Rex, or Antigone* by Sophocles
   >
   > *Medea, Alcestis or The Trojan Women* by Euripedes

2. Construct a mask similar to the ones used in the ancient Greek theatre. Explain to the class the character's personality, social position, and age as symbolized in the mask.

3. Prepare a poster (22" x 24" minimum) which illustrates the major features of a typical Greek theatre.

4. Prepare a poster (22" x 24" minimum) which illustrates a typical costume for an actor during the Golden Age of Greece.

5. Draw a map of ancient Greece on a poster board (22" x 24"). Show the major geographic features as well as political entities (cities, regions, etc.).

CHAPTER FOUR
IMPROVISATION

To improvise is to act without benefit of written dialog. It's sometimes described as ad-libbing, or just making it up as you go along. Improvisation leads a triple life in the theatre. Sometimes it is used as a specific tool by the director during rehearsals for a play. The director might ask members of the cast to act out a scene which is not part of the script — perhaps something that happened before the action of the play begins, or something that takes place off-stage. The purpose of this kind of improvisation is to develop a more complete characterization and a better understanding of the relationships between characters in the play.

Improvisational comedy has become widely known through such groups as Second City, and the television show, *An Evening at the Improv*. In this kind of improvisation, cast members often take suggestions from the audience, then depend on their quick wits — and their long hours of working together — to create an instant comedy sketch. This is riskier than we might suspect. When you improvise like this in front of an audience, it's certain that some scenes will work better than others, and that some will be real turkeys. Television shows are only interested in broadcasting the successful pieces, so those who have never attended in person tend to have the unrealistic idea that every sketch is a roaring success.

Lastly, and of most immediate concern to us, improvisation can be used as a technique to learn acting. We will spend several hours learning how to use a specific form of improvisation that is designed to help student actors become exciting to watch. It develops your ability to be truly alive onstage, responding to what is said and done by the other character(s) without any preconceived ideas about what should happen in the scene. Don't worry if you have trouble "getting it" right away. Most actors have difficulty when first learning this particular technique.

Preparing an Improvisation

As usual, before we can begin the actual exercise, we must take some time to learn the rules. And a big part of learning the rules is understanding the meanings of the words used. Take your time reading this section. Make sure you understand what each term means, and how you will use it in preparing your improvisation.

The important terms for your first try at this kind of improvisation are:

who

when

where

independent activity

objective

conflict

enter

discovered

props

You will work with a partner on this exercise. You and your partner must agree on the who, when, and where. Let's take them one at a time.

Decide on *who* you are. It's probably easiest to begin by *naming the relationship* between the two characters (brothers, mother-daughter, boss-employee, neighbors, husband-wife...almost any relationship is acceptable as long as the two people are not strangers with nothing in common). But naming the relationship is not enough. You must supply some *details* about the relationship. How old are the sisters? How do they get along? If they are adults, how did they get along when they were younger? What did (do) they fight about? Or, how long have they been married? Do they still love each other? Do they have children? Has either been married before? What do they argue about? Be as specific as possible.

> **Improvisation is used three ways in the theatre: as a rehearsal technique, as a form of instant entertainment, and as an excellent tool for developing in student actors a sense of reality on-stage.**

Next, you and your partner will decide on *when* the scene takes place. Again, be specific. Decide on the time of day, day of the week and month, and the year. This is important, because people react differently at 5:00 AM on Christmas morning than they do at 8:00 PM on the Fourth of July, and many people are affected by the work/school week — weekends are different from weekdays. And of course, people in 1869 might respond differently than people in 1569, 1939, or 1989.

Where does the scene take place? Be specific. If it's in a living room, where is the house located? Suburbs, inner city, rural area? Is it a house or an apartment? Large or small? New or old? What part of the country (or the world) is the house in? A cold place like Anchorage, Alaska — or in the heat of Miami, Florida? New York City or Los Angeles? New Orleans, Louisiana — or Benson, Arizona?

You and your partner will have different responsibilities in getting the improvisation started. One of you will be discovered. That is, you will already be on-stage when the scene begins. The other will enter the scene by coming in from off-stage. Decide which of you will be discovered and which will enter.

At this point in the process, you and your partner must *stop* talking to each other. It's important that your partner not know exactly what to expect when the scene starts, so don't share what you decide next.

If you are being discovered on-stage, decide on an *independent activity*. This is something you are doing that is, in all likelihood, unrelated to the scene. The activity must involve you both mentally and physically, and you must have an important reason (and perhaps a deadline) for completing the task. In other words, you must be able to believe that the task is urgent. One other thing: no imaginary props are allowed. Props are objects (usually small) used by actors on-stage. Things like a deck of cards, a briefcase, a telephone, a vase of flowers, or a box of matches are props. For this exercise, you must have real props. That is, if your independent activity consists of memorizing the Gettysburg Address for a school final project that's due in forty-five minutes (and your recitation of it will determine whether you pass or fail the course), you must have a copy of the Gettysburg Address — and you must really work at memorizing it!

If you are entering from off-stage, you must decide on a different kind of objective. You must enter the stage wanting something, and knowing why you want it. In these early exercises, you must want some tangible object, something that your partner can actually put into your hand (a pencil, for example, or a shoelace, or a key, or a book, or a....). Your reason for wanting whatever it is must be important and urgent. In one of the best improvisations I've seen, a student "neighbor" (male) came in demanding pantyhose, because he was taking his unconscious and possibly dying child to the hospital when the fan-belt of his car broke, and he wanted to use the pantyhose as a temporary substitute!

Now you are ready to improvise. You and your partner have created a fertile ground for conflict: two specific characters, in a specific place, at a specific time, each of whom has a specific objective unknown to the other. Without conflict there can be no drama. Without conflict there can be no good acting.

Performing an Improvisation

Now this is going to seem perverse, but the worst thing you can do when you perform an improvisation of this kind is *act*. Instead, you must simply *do*. Why? Because if you're acting, you'll be likely to concern yourself with such things as a time limit for your scene. Or you'll try to determine in advance how the scene should end. These concepts may be important when you're writing a script, but they destroy an improvisation.

Remember that the idea here is to be alive and awake-in-the-moment while you are on-stage. Spontaneity will die if you concern yourself with anything other than your who, when, where, what-you-want-and-why-you-want-it.

As for time limit: there is none. One of the worst things you can do is to drag a scene out, stay on-stage and keep talking because you feel you must act. Consider this real-life example:

> You have finally worked up your courage to ask a big favor of your parents. When you walk into the room, you discover that your parents are scolding your younger brother or sister, saying such things as, "I never did things like that when I was your age! You kids nowadays are all spoiled rotten!"

Do you interrupt to ask if you can have $500 for a trip to the beach? Certainly not! You can tell that your chances of success are very small, and you probably try to get out of the room without attracting attention to yourself!

Then how do you tell when a scene is over? It's over when you either get what you want, or when you give up trying to get it and leave the scene.

But who "wins" in an improvisation? It depends on the situation. In the real-life scene above, your behavior as well as the outcome might have been different if what you came in to say was, "Quick! I need a blanket and the first aid kit! There's been an accident in the street!"

The only "theatrical" concern you need have is for the arrangement of furniture on the stage before you begin. You and your partner should quickly arrange a few chairs, a table, a stool — whatever is handy on the stage — into a semblance of the location you picked for your scene. Then the one who enters should leave the stage, while the one who is discovered begins the independent activity.

A word of caution: *don't feel too safe on-stage.* If you and your partner have prepared correctly, and you are both alive and awake in the moment, the conflict may become more real than you bargained for. While it is never permissible to injure another actor, and although the teacher will yell "Freeze" if it looks like things are getting out of hand, it is your responsibility to duck if your partner starts swinging!

Exercises:

1. On a sheet of notebook paper, list the names of ten relationships you and a partner might use in an improvisation. Select one from your list and write out some details of the background of the two people. Write at least half a page of details.

2. Choose a character from your list of relationships. Describe an independent activity for the character in each of the following situations in this year:
   a. Just before dark on a cold January day in a mountain cabin.

   b. Noon, August 1, on the front porch of a small house in Tulsa.

   Describe an appropriate independent activity for the same situations in the same months but one hundred years ago.

3. Choose a partner, prepare and perform an improvisation as described in this chapter.

4. Add the element of emotion to the preparation of your improv. Learn and practice the emotional preparation technique as explained by your teacher.

5. Choose a new partner, prepare and perform an improvisation. This time, the objective of the entering character can be something intangible.

CHAPTER FIVE

BASIC STAGECRAFT

The visual impact of a play, how it looks to the audience, is determined in large measure by the work of designers and craftsmen in the areas of scenery, costumes, and lighting. The designer's work is essentially done when the director approves the final sketches, watercolor renderings, and/or models. In the professional theatre the designer often doesn't even do the drafting of working drawings; a draftsman is hired to translate the sketches into scale drawings. Then it's up to the master carpenter and his crew to transform those sketches into full-sized working scenery.

Of course, nobody expects you to become a stage carpenter just to pass a beginning drama class, but there are at least two reasons for learning a little about stagecraft. First, all play productions need people who know the basics of set construction — the ability to build a flat correctly and do other simple tasks involving saws, hammers, nails, screws, and drills is a proven method of "paying your dues," making yourself an important part of any theatre group. Once you've been accepted as a valuable member of the team, you'll be asked to do other, more glamorous jobs. Second, confidence in using simple tools is a valuable asset in your life outside the theatre. Being able to repair a broken chair, or install your own garbage disposal, or just hang a picture straight will simplify your life in many ways — and save you some money, too!

Tools and Hardware

The dazzling scenery of Broadway or Las Vegas often involves fairly "high tech" tools, hardware, and techniques. Most high schools, however, lack the financial resources and technical expertise to take advantage of the latest advances in scenery construction. In most high school and community theatres, where creativity takes the place of big budgets, scenery is built using simple hand tools and traditional construction techniques.

The tools and hardware needed for scenery can be divided into three categories: measuring, cutting, and assembling.

Measuring Tools

Stagecraft involves two kinds of measurements: lengths and angles. Four tools suffice for most of this work.

Steel tape: This is the familiar tape measure found in most home tool boxes or junk drawers. A plastic or metal case contains a coiled ribbon of steel. Available in lengths from 6' to 100', shorter models have spring-loaded blades that automatically retract, while longer tapes must be wound into the case with a built-in crank. The metal tab on the end can be hooked over one end of an object to be measured, making it possible for one person to measure long "stuff" accurately.

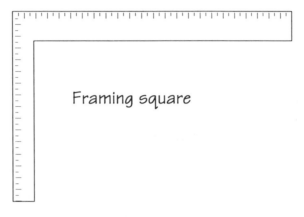

Steel tape

Framing Square: An L-shaped piece of steel or aluminum marked as a ruler. One side is 24" long, the other only 16". Frequently contains markings for determining a 45º angle. It's used for measuring short distances, for drawing straight lines, and for assembling flats, for example, with square (90º) corners.

Framing square

Combination square: This is a metal ruler, 12" long, with a funny handle that makes the whole thing look like a make-believe pistol. The ruler is attached to the handle by friction, and can be adjusted by loosening a knurled knob. Used for measuring short things, and for marking lumber for accurate cutting at 90º or 45º angles. Some combination squares also contain a bubble level (for making sure that an object is parallel or perpendicular to the floor), and a scribe (sort of a metal "pencil" for marking lines on lumber).

Combination square

Chalk line: This isn't a measuring tool, but it's handy for marking long straight lines for cutting plywood, for example, or when you need to paint a long straight line on the scenery. It's a metal case full of powdered pigment (dry paint) in which a long piece of string is wound on a spindle. The string has a hook on the end for

single-handed use. When the string is pulled from the case, stretched taut across a surface, and "snapped," a perfectly straight line is marked on the surface. This tool can also be used to make sure that a wall, door, or other object is plumb, or perpendicular to the ground. When the string is unwound and the hook is held at the top of the wall, the weight of the case makes the string hang exactly perpen-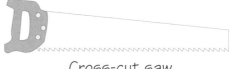 Chalk line / plumb bob
dicular to the ground. The scenery can then be adjusted until its edge is also perpendicular.

Cutting Tools

Lumber, cardboard, and fabric are the most often cut materials in basic stagecraft, although it is occasionally necessary to cut a length of pipe or other metal. Four kinds of saws and one knife will handle most of these chores.

Cross-cut saw: This is the traditional hand saw used for cutting boards to the right length. With a little practice, it provides quick, clean cuts at a variety of angles — and without an extension cord! It's called a cross-cut saw because the teeth are sized and angled for cutting across the

Cross-cut saw

grain of the wood. A *rip saw* looks very much the same, but the teeth are spaced for cutting with the grain rather than across it.

Hack saw: This saw is used for cutting metal (pipes, bolts, etc.) and certain kinds of plastic. It has very fine teeth, and cutting through a steel pipe with one provides very good exercise.

Hack saw

Jig saw: Sometimes called a Sabre saw (a trade name), this electric saw can be fitted with a variety of blades for cutting plywood, wallboard, plastics, even cardboard. The small size of the blade makes it possible to cut curves, so this saw is often used in cutting out patterns or complicated shapes.

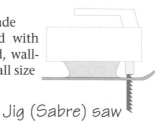
Jig (Sabre) saw

Circular saw: An other electric saw, but this one is used for making straight cuts. It's sometimes called a Skil saw (another trade name).

Circular saw (Skil saw)

Utility knife

Utility knife: Also known as a matte knife, this is the tool of choice for cutting cardboard, Upson board, and other lightweight materials. Some models have retractable blades.

Assembling Tools

The tools in this category are used to fasten things together. Of course, they are also used to take things apart, but not until they've been put together!

Hammers: There are many kinds of hammers and mallets designed for specific uses. The two most often used in basic stagecraft are the curved-claw hammer and the straight-claw or rip hammer. Standard claw hammers have a 16-ounce head. The difference between the two is in the amount of curve in the claw part. The more pronounced curve of the curved-claw hammer makes for greater ease in pulling out nails, while the straighter claw of the rip hammer is useful in prying apart two pieces of wood.

Rip hammer

Curved-claw hammer

Open-end adjustable wrench: Commonly referred to as a Crescent wrench (a trade name), this is one of the most useful tools in the shop. It can tighten and loosen bolts and nuts of various sizes. A tight fit is achieved by turning a knurled worm gear, which moves one jaw of the wrench relative to the other. Lengths from 6" to 12" are most commonly found in theatre shops.

Open-end adjustable wrench (Crescent wrench)

Pliers: Ordinary pliers, or slip-joint pliers, can be used for cutting heavy wire and for general twisting and turning chores, or any time a strong grip on a small object is important. They can also be used for pulling out small nails. They are called slip-joint pliers because the pivot point can be shifted, allowing the handles to stay closer together when grasping a larger object. Needle-nose pliers are handy for grasping smaller objects.

Slip-joint pliers

Electric drill: The variable-speed, reversing electric drill has become one of the most indispensable tools in the theatre shop. Besides drilling holes, it is used for driving and removing screws. Cordless drills are available, but affordable ones don't have enough power for sustained use.

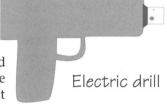

Electric drill

Screwdrivers: Although there are many specialty screw and nut drivers, only two are commonly needed in basic set construction. The slotted screwdriver is used for tightening (or loosening) screws or bolts with slotted heads. There is an almost irresistible urge to use this tool for other purposes, such as removing staples (okay), opening paint cans (probably okay), and prying apart pieces of lumber (not a good idea). Remember, there are such things as putty knives, chisels, and crowbars. Phillips head screwdrivers are used when the screw or bolt has a phillips head (when you look straight down at the head of the screw, it looks like it has a cross cut into it).

Slotted screwdriver

Phillips-head screwdriver

Staple gun

Staple gun: Whether mechanical or electric, this is a handy tool for attaching muslin to flats and for a hundred other fastening tasks that come along during the preparation for a play. They are quite powerful, so be careful not to staple your finger to the floor.

Electric staple gun

Hardware

The hardware needed for basic stagecraft consists mostly of various kinds of fasteners. Several types of nails, screws, bolts, nuts, and washers are commonly used in the assembly of basic scenic units. These, along with several types of hinges used for fastening units together, are explained in this section.

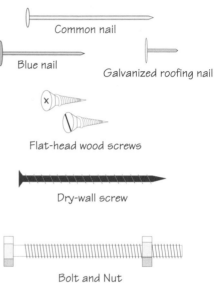

Common nail

Blue nail

Galvanized roofing nail

Flat-head wood screws

Dry-wall screw

Bolt and Nut

Nails: Various types of nails have long been the most common fastener in basic stagecraft and general carpentry. Common or box nails are used in joining together two scenic units and in attaching diagonal braces to platform legs. Cement-coated nails are available, and they hold much tighter — but they are extremely difficult to remove and almost always destroy the lumber. Blue nails, also called lath nails, are commonly used in the construction of flats. They look slightly blue, like a gun barrel. Galvanized roofing nails are short and fat, with large heads. They are handy for attaching corrugated cardboard to platforms, because the large head makes it easier to avoid "breaking the skin" of the cardboard.

Wood screws: Joints fastened with screws are stronger than nailed joints. Unlike a bolt, a screw drills its own hole (except for a small pilot hole) through the materials to be fastened, and the length of the screw must be less than the combined thickness of the pieces being joined. Flat-head wood screws are used for attaching hinges and other metal fixtures to wooden scenery.

Drywall screws: The development of the drywall screw (originally used in the interior finishing of homes and offices) has provided a great advance in basic stagecraft. These relatively inexpensive screws are available in a variety of lengths, and, combined with the reversible electric drill, have almost entirely replaced nails in most applications in many theatre shops. The construction of platforms and the attaching of various braces to scenery, as well as the fastening together of two scenic units, are made much easier and faster.

An additional advantage is that it is simple to remove the screws when striking the set, with little damage to the scenery.

Bolts and Nuts: Bolts provide the strongest possible joints for basic stagecraft, and are commonly used for attaching legs to platforms and other applications where strength is important for safety. Bolts are threaded metal cylinders, and they are available in many types and sizes. One of the most common has a hexagonal head, requiring a wrench for tightening or loosening. Using a bolt requires that a hole be drilled through the materials to be fastened. The bolt is inserted through the hole, and a nut is tightened on the end. Often, a flat washer is placed between the piece and the nut.

Hinges: Three types of hinges are commonly used in basic stagecraft. A hinge consists of two metal pieces with interlocking "cars," and a cylindrical pin which holds the two pieces together while allowing them to pivot. A loose-pin hinge permits the removal of the pin, allowing the hinge (and the two pieces it's attached to) to be separated without removing the screws from the hinge. A tight-pin hinge has a permanently installed pin, removable only by cutting.

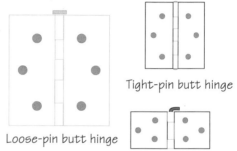

Tight-pin butt hinge

Loose-pin butt hinge

Loose-pin back-flap hinge

The loose-pin back-flap hinge is used for temporarily attaching two pieces of scenery together, as when a step unit must be attached to a platform during a scene but moved as a separate unit between scenes. A loose-pin butt hinge is used for hanging a full-size door, and a tight-pin butt hinge is used for cabinet doors and other such small applications.

The Flat: A Basic Unit of Scenery

A flat is a wooden framework covered with cloth. Its ease of construction and light weight have made it a standard in theatrical scenery.

Materials

The frame for a flat is constructed of 1" x 3" pine. (Note: Lumber is sized before the final milling process, so the actual measurement is always smaller than the stated size. 1" x 3" lumber typically measures ⅝" or ¹¹⁄₁₆" x 2⅝" or 2¹¹⁄₁₆". Lumber is sold in various grades. Clear is the best grade, with no knots or imperfections, but d-Select, the second-best grade, is fine for this use. Unfortunately, both these grades have become prohibitively expensive, so you will probably want to use #2, which is the third best grade, and has many knots; if possible, you should go to the lumber yard and hand pick the pieces you want to use, minimizing the amount of waste. Otherwise, you'll need to order approximately 40-50% more than the actual amount needed.) Corner braces are made of 1" x 2" pine. The joints of a flat are held together by pieces of ¼" plywood. (Note: Plywood is sold in 4' x 8' sheets, graded according to the quality of each of the two surfaces. AC shop grade plywood [one good side] is good enough for most scenery uses.)

You will also need a supply of blue nails (the shortest ones you can buy), and staples (¼" or ⅚₆" is plenty long enough for the "leg" of the staples) for your staple gun. Also, you'll want to cover the flat and prepare it for painting. The fabric used to cover flats is called unbleached muslin, available in widths up to 108".

Tools

      steel tape measure

      framing square

      combination square

      hammer(s)

      saw (cross-cut or circular)

      safety goggles

      pencil or scribe

      staple gun

Construction

Determine the size of the finished flat by consulting the designer's elevations. (For the purposes of this explanation, assume that the flat is to be 12' tall x 4' wide.) On the illustration on page 33, notice that the rails are the only parts of the flat which measure the full length or width of the flat. That's why these are measured and cut first.

Use the steel tape to mark the length of a rail (4' - 0") on the lumber, then use the combination square to draw a perpendicular line across the lumber. (Note: Remember that when you cut the lumber, you will lose a small amount, the *kerf*, equal to the thickness of the saw blade, to sawdust. This means you can't mark consecutive lengths down the piece of lumber; you can, however, mark one length from each end.)

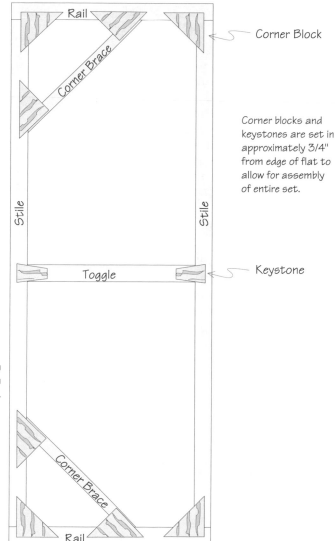

Corner Block

Corner blocks and keystones are set in approximately 3/4" from edge of flat to allow for assembly of entire set.

Keystone

Note that direction of visible plywood grain goes across butt joints.

Standard Theatrical Flat

Stiles, rails, toggle, of 1"x3" white pine;
corner braces of 1"x2" white pine;
corner blocks and keystones of 1/4" plywood

Saw the lumber to the marked length, being sure to keep the saw just on the "outside" of the line marked so that the finished piece won't be too short. Measure, mark and cut the other rail.

Here's how to determine the correct length of the stiles without measuring the width of the lumber being used, then adding and subtracting fractions from the 12' height of the flat: lay the two rails flat on the floor, right next to each other. Then lay a fresh piece at a right angle to them, with the end of the piece against the rails. Measure the height of the flat along the new piece by including the two rails. This will automatically deduct the correct amount from the length of the stile.

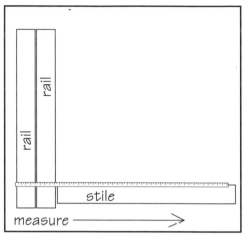

Measure and mark both stiles as described above. After cutting the stiles, use them to "measure" the correct length of the toggle. Cut the toggle.

Lay the pieces on the floor in the shape of the flat. Flats are assembled using butt joints. This simply means that the end of one piece butts up against the edge of another piece. The two pieces are held together by nailing a piece of plywood over the joint.

Most theatre shops keep a supply of precut corner blocks and keystones. A corner block can be made easily by first cutting 12" squares, then splitting the squares diagonally. Keystones should be cut from strips of plywood approximately 3" wide.

Use the framing square to make sure that one corner is perfectly square. Set a corner block over the joint, making sure that the direction of the wood grain on the surface of the plywood goes across the joint. (This is because ¼" plywood has only three layers, or plies, of wood and is stronger in the direction of grain on the two surfaces.) Use a scrap piece of 1" x 3", on edge, to establish the correct inset for the corner block — the scrap should be flush with the edge of the flat, and the corner block pushed up against the 1" x 3" scrap. Then drive two blue nails into the plywood on either side of the joint. On

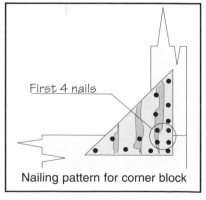

Nailing pattern for corner block

one side of the joint, the nails should be driven into the flat itself, but not all the way in. Check to be sure the joint is square before driving in the other two. These four nails will hold the joint square (unless you kick one of the pieces) until you can complete nailing on the corner block.

The rest of the nails should be put in according to the pattern on page 34. Start at each corner, then work in a zigzag pattern back toward the joint. Do not drive any nail all the way in.

Work your way around the flat, completing one corner at a time. After the fourth corner is joined, make this final check: use the steel tape to measure the two diagonals of the flat — if the flat is square and true, the two diagonals will be the same length. If the diagonals are not the same length, one or more corners will have to be taken apart and re-joined. (That's why the nails are not driven all the way in.)

When the corners are square, install the toggle at the midpoint of the flat. (Very tall flats may require more than one toggle.) Corner braces should be installed last. These are pieces of 1" x 2" pine (1" x 3" will do, but it's heavier) with ends cut at a 45° angle. It's important for the structural rigidity of the flat that both corner braces be installed on the same side of the flat. Don't forget to use the 1" x 3" scrap to inset the keystones on the toggle and corner blocks on the braces.

When the assembly is complete, the nails need to be driven all the way in and clinched (bent over or flattened out on the pointed end). Clinching makes the joint stronger by increasing the holding power of the nails.

The best way to do this is with a clinch plate, a piece of steel plate placed under the joint while you drive the nail heads flush with the surface of the plywood. If your framing square is steel (aluminum is too soft) it will serve as a clinch plate. If no clinch plate is available, it will be necessary to first drive the nail heads flush (working on a wooden floor is probably best, because the nail points will create tiny chips and pits in a concrete floor), then turn the flat over onto its back and use the hammer to flatten the nail points. In any event, it's important to turn the flat onto its back to make sure all the nail points are flattened out flush with the face of the flat.

Covering the Flat

Take care when you are covering the flat, because the final appearance of the scenery can be ruined by a sloppy job at this step. There are several ways to cover a flat; here's a favorite.

Lay the flat face-up on the floor or work table. Place the muslin loosely on top so that it overlaps all four edges of the flat. Tear the muslin so that it is the same size as the flat, or only slightly bigger. (Save all the muslin scraps except for the strips torn from the edges of the fabric where it is woven back on itself [the selvage] — they're always useful for something!)

Staples should be placed near the inside edge of the stile so that the muslin can be easily glued to the wood when stapling is completed. Begin stapling at the center of one stile, near the toggle. Alternate sides of the flat, working your way outward from your first staple on each side, as shown in the drawing below. Pull the fabric tight be-tween staples on the same side, approximately nine inches apart.

How tight you pull the fabric *across* the flat depends on what kind of muslin you are using and on the size of the flat. If you are using nonflameproofed muslin, leave the fabric slack enough so that it sags to the floor or work table surface in the center of the flat. Flameproofed muslin must be pulled tighter because it will not tighten up as much when the sizing is applied to the flat. Narrow flats also require less slack, too, because the proportion of unsupported fabric is much smaller.

WHAT ARE SCISSORS FOR?

Why not use scissors or a knife to cut the muslin? Why do we tear it? Because muslin, like almost all woven fabrics, tears along a thread, tearing is one way to make sure your piece has straight sides and square corners — without having to mark the lines for cutting. Also, torn edges will unravel or fray slightly, and this is an advantage in scene painting, making it easier to dis-guise the edges so the audience won't see them.

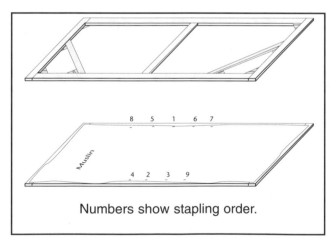

Numbers show stapling order.

The ends of the flat are stapled one at a time. Begin in the middle, then work outwards to the corners. If there is excess fabric, ease it (divide the excess evenly) between staples.

Using a paint brush, apply a mixture of equal parts glue and water. Flip the edge of the muslin back, paint the wood with the glue mixture, then replace the muslin and add more glue, smoothing the fabric so there are no wrinkles.

When the glue has dried, paint the surface of the flat with a sizing solution. Sizing is a mixture of water and glue (about four or five parts water to one part glue) or dissolved starch. You may wish to add a very small amount of pigment to the sizing to make it easier to see where you've applied the sizing and where you haven't. The sizing will dry faster if the flat is leaned against a wall to allow air circulation beneath it.

If everything has been done correctly, the flat will dry tight and smooth, with no wrinkles anywhere. If otherwise, next time adjust the tightness of the muslin when you staple.

Exercises:

1. Create a large poster–sized display of various types and sizes of nails and their common uses. Be sure to include an explanation of the "penny" system of measuring nails. This may involve a trip to the library as well as to the hardware store.

2. Create a series of three 9" x 12" or 11" x 14" posters relating to shop safety. Include at least two of the following areas of concern: wearing safety goggles, using the proper tool for the job, cleaning up the work area often, not leaving tools on top of ladders, not treating tools as toys.

3. Build a miniature flat measuring 1'–0" x 2'–0". Use 1x3 stock and 1/4" plywood, along with blue nails. (You will need to alter the nailing pattern because of the reduced size of the flat.) You need not cover the flat.

4. Write a report on the composition and uses of plywood (especially ¼" and ¾"), explaining both why it is strong and why difficulties may arise in joining plywood with nails and screws.

CHAPTER SIX

YOUR VOCAL INSTRUMENT

An actor has only two tools with which to reach the audience: body and voice. It's imperative that both be trained to be flexible and strong, able to fulfill the demands of any director and any role. This chapter will give you a basic understanding of how the voice is produced and examine the range of possibilities in vocal characterization open to the actor.

How the Voice Works

The ability to speak, and to express such a wide range of ideas through speech, is a distinctly human characteristic. The speech mechanism itself, though, is composed of various parts of our bodies which have other uses.

These other uses are actually more important to our physical survival than speech. Our diaphragm, lungs, and nasal passages are vital for breathing. Our teeth, lips, and tongue are important for eating and swallowing. This is why speech is often called an *overlaid function*: the use of our lips, teeth, lungs, and so on for speech is laid over their primary functions.

Proper appreciation of our vocal instrument begins with learning the physical mechanisms by which it is produced. Discovering how our voice works will allow us to exercise it more effectively, extending its range without damaging it.

The Four Processes of Speech

Four steps are involved in the production of speech: respiration, phonation, resonation, and articulation. Let's take a look at the parts of our bodies needed for each process.

Respiration, or breathing, is something that we all do. As a matter of fact, we're all pretty good at it, or we wouldn't be here! Breathing is so natural that most people never think about it, but student actors can't afford not to think about it.

In its simplest terms, breathing is the process by which air is taken into the lungs so that our blood can receive the oxygen we need to live. The lungs are not muscles, and there are no muscles attached to them, so how, you may ask, is the air "taken in"?

Our lungs rest inside our chest cavity, or *thorax,* surrounded by the rib cage and bounded at the bottom by the diaphragm. (The diaphragm is a large, strong muscle that separates the thorax from the abdomen.) Air is

39

drawn into the lungs by increasing the size of the chest cavity, which reduces the relative air pressure inside the thorax and causes air from outside to rush in until the pressure is equalized.

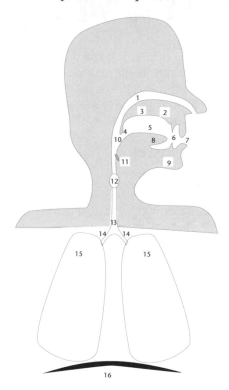

1. Nasal cavity
2. Hard palate
3. Soft palate
4. Uvula
5. Oral cavity
6. Teeth
7. Lips
8. Tongue
9. Lower jaw
10. Pharynx
11. Epiglottis
12. Larynx
13. Trachea
14. Bronchial tubes
15. Lungs
16. Diaphragm

There are three ways to increase the size of the chest cavity.

1) The **clavicles** (collar bones) can be elevated, which usually causes a corresponding elevation of the shoulders.

2) The **rib cage** can be expanded, rather like an old-fashioned bellows.

3) The **diaphragm** can be contracted, forcing the abdominal organs downward and/or outward.

Clavicular breathing works wonderfully well — if all you need to do is stay alive. But the actor needs a large supply of air for making long speeches, and the limited movement of the clavicles means that only a small amount of air is taken into the top part of the lungs.

Rib-cage breathing is more efficient than clavicular breathing, because the rib cage can be expanded more than the clavicles can be raised. This draws a greater amount of air into the lungs, but not as much or as deeply as the third alternative, diaphragmatic breathing.

Contracting the diaphragm draws a large quantity of air deep into the lungs. This provides an actor (or a singer, or a clarinetist, etc.) with a large supply of air. This air, supported on exhalation by the strength of the diaphragm, enables the actor to make long speeches without gasping for breath.

It is a sad fact that although everyone is born a natural diaphragmatic breather, most of us seem to forget how to do it — at least while we're awake and vertical! To test yourself for diaphragmatic breathing, place the palm of your hand over your stomach with your thumb resting just below your *sternum* (breastbone). When you inhale (breathe in), your hand should be pushed out, and when you exhale (breathe out), your hand should move in towards your spine.

If your diaphragm doesn't seem to work, don't despair. Try this: lie down on your back with a heavy book on your stomach. As you relax, the book should begin a slow rise and fall, in time with your breathing. Carefully remove the book, replacing it with your hand. Allow your hand to rise and fall several times, then — slowly and carefully — try standing up while keeping the movement of your diaphragm the same.

If even that doesn't seem to work, then it's worth trying this "psychological trick." All of us breathe diaphragmatically when we sleep, so perhaps we can fool our subconscious into thinking that what we were going to do anyway is really practice for drama class! After you go to bed at night, just before you drift off to sleep, lie on your back and get your diaphragmatic breathing started. Then tell yourself something like this: "Now I'm going to practice breathing with my diaphragm for eight hours, and when I wake up

This is probably the first time you've had homework assigned to be done *while you sleep!*

and get out of bed it will be easier to breathe diaphragmatically than it was today." This is one of those efforts to harness the power of the subconscious mind; if it works, great! And if it doesn't, nothing has been lost.

Phonation, making a sound, is the second process in speaking. Sound is created by vibration, but what part of our speech mechanism provides the vibration?

The air taken into our lungs is pushed out through the *bronchial tubes* and *trachea*. As it passes through the *larynx*, or voice box (or Adam's apple), the vocal folds are brought close enough together that the passing stream of air causes them to vibrate. This vibration is a sound, just as the vibrating of

41

a trumpet player's lips, or a guitar string, or even a plucked rubber band is a sound.

The larynx is a small bundle of cartilage, muscles, tendons, and other tissues, including the *vocal folds*. It is really a marvel of miniaturization, the way the tiny pieces of cartilage pivot, stretching the vocal folds and bringing them close together, then regulating the amount of tension to create high pitches and low pitches. But the sound it creates is very soft and quiet; it can hardly be heard unless the room is very quiet.

Resonation is the third process of speaking. Just as a trumpeter's lips need a trumpet and a guitar string needs a sound box or electronic pick-up, the sound created by the vocal folds needs to be made louder and stronger. This function is served by three parts of our speech mechanism: the *pharynx*, the *oral cavity*, and the *nasal cavity*.

The pharynx is the large open area at the back of your mouth (or the top of your throat, depending on how you want to look at it). The oral cavity is the mouth, and the nasal cavity is the air passage from the pharynx to the nose.

The size and shape of these open spaces provides each of us with a unique "voice print." They are what gives us recognizably different voices. And what does this mean for actors? How can we take advantage of this fact to acquire a rich and resonant voice?

Generally speaking, the larger the resonator, the larger and more resonant will be the sound. Although we are born with our hard and soft palates, and the size and shape of our pharynx and nasal cavity are genetically determined, knowledge and training can make a difference. The pharynx can be made larger (more resonant) by learning to relax the muscles of the throat. The oral cavity can be made larger by simply opening the mouth wider when speaking, avoiding the most common American speech problem, tight jaw.

Articulation is the final process of speaking. Through the processes of respiration, phonation, and resonation, we have created a sound loud enough to be heard. But without articulation, breaking the sound into meaningful units and patterns, we would only be able to utter grunts and shouts. The seven articulators (*teeth, lips, tongue, lower jaw, hard palate, soft palate,* and *epiglottis*) shape the sound into syllables and words that enable us to convey a wide range of thoughts and emotions to our audience, whether in the theatre or in our living room.

The articulators are used in various combinations. The tongue and lower jaw are responsible for most of the vowel sounds. Try saying the vowels sounds in *beet, bit, bet, bat* for example, and notice how your mouth opens wider and your tongue moves from high to low in the front of your mouth.

The lips form the plosives *b* and *p*, teeth and lower lip combine for the fricatives *f* and *v*, tongue and teeth are responsible for the sounds of *th* in think and breathe. The tongue and the hard palate get together on *t* and *d* (and come close for *s* and *z*), and the soft palate kisses the back of the tongue for *k* and *g*.

The Four Properties of Tone

The sound of our voice can be altered at our discretion in four different ways: *strength*, *pitch*, *time*, and *quality*. An actor must have a wide range of choices in each category to provide the widest range of characterizations.

Strength

"Project!" shouts the director. "Remember the deaf old lady in the back row!" The property of voice commonly referred to as loudness or volume is better described by the term strength. How much sound we produce is governed by the amount of air we push past our vocal folds, and the support of the diaphragm is essential. It is very important to keep in mind that our goal is *Strength Without Strain*. Proper relaxation of the throat muscles combined with support from the diaphragm will permit

Strength Without **STRAIN** is the secret of a healthy and powerful voice.

us to have a very strong voice without getting hoarse — as we tend to do when we yell for victory at a football game, for example.

A convenient system for measuring strength is important, because it will allow us to understand each other when we talk about how strongly a particular line should be delivered. The system of numbers used is not scientific — we won't need an audiometer or decibel meter

Vocal Strengths

Level	Description
1-	very soft whisper — no phonation
	projection line
1	stage whisper
1+	quiet or hushed conversation
2-	normal conversation
2	heated conversation
2+	calling to another room
3-	calling across campus
3	strongest possible shout

(the decibel is the unit of loudness) — but it has worked well in many classes and rehearsals over the years.

The projection line represents the level of strength below which the actor can't be heard. Because theatres vary in size, shape, and other acoustical properties, the projection line will differ from one theatre to another. Even the same theatre is different acoustically when it's full of people: the people and their clothing absorb more sound waves, and they make more noise just shifting in their seats, sniffling, sneezing, and coughing. For these reasons, it's important for an actor to test each theatre under varying conditions by having a reliable listener (a drama teacher or director, for example) sit near the back of the house while the actor speaks from the stage.

Pitch

Most of us understand that pitch is associated with music — that a flute is higher pitched than a tuba, and that singing requires close attention to pitch. Although most people make use of only a small part of it, the human voice is capable of a wide range of pitches.

The pitch of a sound is determined by the speed of the vibration producing the sound — the faster the vibration, the higher the pitch. The speed of vibration is largely determined by the thickness, tension, and length of the vibrating body. In a stringed instrument, for example, an "open" string vibrates at a pitch determined by its length, thickness and how tightly it is stretched. When the string is "shortened" by holding it down to the fingerboard, the pitch rises.

Rising inflections

Falling inflections

Circumflex inflections

The thickness of our vocal folds is determined by genetics and gender. We control the length and "tightness" by making tiny adjustments in the larynx.

Inflection is the word we use to describe the variations in pitch during speech, most commonly during one sentence or one word. A sentence or a word can have a rising inflection, a falling inflection, or a circumflex inflection. The voice of a person with a limited pitch range, unable to use a wide variety of inflections, is

44

often described as a monotone.

As an aspiring actor, you should work to develop your total pitch range until you are able to be expressive (not monotonous) in each of three mini-ranges: high, medium, and low. One of the best ways to extend your range is by studying singing. Private lessons are excellent, but a school or church choir is a good substitute, offering both a low price and performance opportunities.

Time

The two parts of our speech that can be timed are the sounds and the silences — the spaces between the sounds. Each of these contributes to the total effect our speech has on the listener. Short sounds combined with short silences creates a very rapid speech, giving our articulators a workout. Long sounds separated by short silences creates a very musical sound, appropriate for classical drama, or any poetic speech. Sometimes, using a long silence places extra emphasis on the sound(s) that follow.

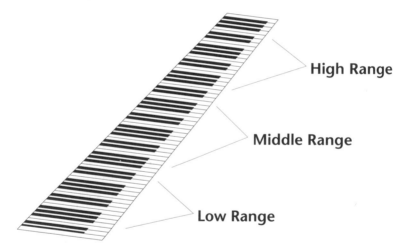

High Range

Middle Range

Low Range

It's important to remember that the audience's perception of how fast an actor speaks is just that: a perception. It often bears little relationship to the actual number of words per minute being spoken. An actor with sloppy articulation or a weak voice will be perceived as "speaking too fast" even when the actual speed is fairly slow.

Quality

We've all experimented with changing our vocal quality — when we make our voices sound "spooky" to play Halloween ghosts, for example. Even whispering is a change in the quality of our vocal tone. The human voice can achieve an infinite number of slightly different qualities, as we know from listening to the wide variety of voices around us, but we will deal with only six basic ones.

The *normal* quality is the one most untrained speakers use in their daily lives. Relatively few people make the best possible use of their resonators for a full, rich voice, and few people sustain the exaggerated use of one tone quality necessary to make them stand out in a crowd.

The *nasal* quality is created by allowing more air than normal to escape through the nose during speech. Spoken English has only three completely nasal sounds: *m, n,* and *-ng.* Most other speech sounds, however, allow a small portion of air (and sound) to escape through the nose. That's why a person's voice sounds different when his nose is plugged (or pinched shut), even when he's not trying to say, "I'b goig dowd towd, Bob. (I'm going downtown, Mom.)"

A nasal quality is generally associated with unpleasant characters, but a little extra nasality can increase the carrying power of your voice for loud shouts across long distances. The amount of air and sound escaping through the nose is regulated by the placement of the *velum,* the back part of the soft palate. If the velum is raised until it touches the back of the throat, it seals off the nasal passages. On the other hand, if it is lowered farther than normal, it creates a nasal tone quality.

The *oral* quality produces a very "light" sound, and is associated with children, very old people, and some foreign dialects. It is produced when most of the resonance of the pharynx is bypassed, allowing almost all resonance to come from the oral cavity. Although it is physiologically incorrect, many actors trying to produce the oral quality find it useful to think of the voice as being "placed" in the front part of the mouth, just behind the teeth.

A *guttural* voice is often described as throaty, raspy, or gravelly. If the oral "voice" is placed in the front of the mouth, then the guttural voice is placed deep in the pharynx. It is often associated with rough–and–tough characters, and certain old men. Care must be taken not to strain the voice when using the guttural quality. The tension in the throat muscles necessary for an extremely guttural quality can result in hoarseness and damage to the vocal folds.

The *aspirate* quality is almost always used in combination with another quality for stage work. A pure aspirate quality requires that phonation not take place, producing a true whisper that is difficult to project to the front rows, let alone to the deaf old lady in the back row! A stage whisper uses another quality, but allows plenty of air to escape "around the edges" of the voice. This creates the psychological effect of a whisper — the need for quiet — but can be heard by the whole audience. An aspirate quality is also useful for playing ghosts and ghouls, as well as certain female roles (such as a

Hollywood starlet of the '50s or '60s). Because of the amount of air being expended without creating extra strength, actors find that using an aspirate quality requires them to breathe more frequently.

The *orotund* quality is defined as the quality which is the richest, fullest, most resonant that the individual can produce. Each person's vocal equipment is determined in large measure by genetics. While there may be some changes through procedures such as orthodontia, improving your tone quality is basically a matter of training the vocal mechanism: learning to relax the throat muscles, loosening and strengthening the jaw muscles, and learning to regulate the placement of the soft palate. A rich and resonant voice is possible for everyone, and it is an asset not only for actors but for people in all walks of life.

Accents and Dialects

Many people have experienced meeting a person new to their town and noticing that the newcomer has an accent. If you live in Tucson or San Francisco or Seattle, you will notice the accents of people who grew up in Alabama, Maine, Brooklyn, or Virginia — not to mention those from Australia, England, France, Germany, Ireland, Scotland, Mexico, Italy...and so on. Even those who have never met somebody with an accent have heard them many times in the movies and on television.

We seldom recognize, however, that *everybody* speaks with an accent! Even though we don't hear ourselves speak with an accent, a person who moves from Tucson to New Orleans or Tallahassee or Montpelier will be recognized as a newcomer as soon as he or she begins to speak. By the same token, residents of Dublin, Ireland, don't hear themselves speaking with an accent or dialect, but would quickly recognize as a newcomer any American speaker.

Our modern age of radio, television, and movies has partially eradicated American regional dialects. Most radio and television newscasters, announcers, and actors speak with a nonregional dialect — you can't tell where they came from. People eager to expand their businesses into other parts of the country or the world can even take classes to get rid of their regional dialects!

Many parts in plays require that the actor speak with a convincing and believable accent other than his or her own. Actors need to be able to sound as if they come from Ireland for plays such as Brian Friel's *Philadelphia, Here I Come,* from London (upper class, Cockney, and one Hungarian, too!) for George Bernard Shaw's *Pygmalion,* and from New Hampshire for Wilder's *Our Town.* Actors also need to sound like they are from nowhere in particular (called standard stage diction) for roles in Chekhov's *The Three Sisters,* Ibsen's *The Wild Duck,* Rostand's *Cyrano de Bergerac* and many others.

Plays originally written in another language — such as the last three mentioned above — are performed without foreign accents, unless one of the characters in the play is supposed to be a foreigner. That is to say, Carlo Goldoni's plays, originally written in Italian, are not done with an Italian accent. His original audience heard the characters speak without accent, so our audiences should, too. Of course, the part of a Frenchman in one of Goldoni's plays would require the use of a French accent now as it did originally.

Learning a New Dialect or Accent

Some lucky actors have a "good ear" for dialects. They can learn a new accent or dialect just by listening to and imitating a person from the same part of the world as the character the actor wants to play. One of the advantages of the revolution in movies and television is that it is quite simple to purchase or rent a video copy of a film whose characters use the dialect in question. Large cities often have diverse populations, making it possible to find and converse with one or more individuals who can serve as models for the appropriate dialect or accent.

For those without such a good ear, or without access to a speaker of the particular dialect or accent they need, there are other ways to learn. Several publishers offer dialect books, and some of them include cassette tapes so that you can hear and repeat individually the specific sound changes required in your new dialect.

Choose a Good Model!

There is a story about a young actor chosen to play the part of an Albanian in a New York show. The actor assured the director that the accent would be "no problem." It seems the actor had met an Albanian fellow who was working at one of those food carts, selling hot dogs. The actor explained that he wouldn't use the accent at rehearsal until he had mastered it, and every day he ate lunch at the same stand, so he could listen and learn. Finally, three days before the show was set to open, the director pushed the actor into using the accent at rehearsal. Afterward, the director complimented the actor on the authenticity of the accent, but asked, "Why does your character suddenly speak with a lisp?" The actor had copied the hot dog seller exactly, including his speech defect!

Elements of Accents and Dialects

Whatever the method you use, you will need to master each of these five elements: vowel changes, consonant changes, inflection patterns, stress patterns, and word choices.

Changes in the sounds of vowels and consonants are important. For example, a British dialect changes the sound of our "can't" into something that sounds as though it would be spelled "cahn't." A German or French accent changes our "this" into something like "zis" or "dis."

Each accent or dialect has its own lilt, or common inflection pattern. A Frenchman speaking English, for example, is apt to bring to English his custom of ending statements with a rising inflection, making it sound like a question to our ears.

Stress patterns vary, too. We say laboratory as "**lab**ratory," while a Londoner might say "la**bo**ratry." British speakers use secondary stress in long words much more frequently than their American counterparts.

Too Much of Good Thing?

Sometimes an actor must sacrifice authenticity in a dialect in order to be understood by the audience. An absolutely true, authentic Cockney accent, for example, can be very difficult to understand — the actor must soften the dialect a bit so that the character still has a Cockney sound but can be enjoyed by the audience.

Word choice is important if you plan to use the accent or dialect for anything other than memorized dialog where a playwright has chosen the words for you. Otherwise you'll need to know whether to call it a gully, a ravine, or an arroyo. Do you greet people with, "Top o' the mornin' to you," or "'ow's yer poor old feet?" Is it a bag or a sack? A wallet or a billfold? A sofa, a couch, a davenport, or a settee?

Learning and using different accents and dialects can make your performance more believable and interesting. It can also be great fun.

Exercises:

1. Demonstrate the use of a range of strengths, pitches, times, and qualities in an oral presentation to the class.

2. Make a working model that shows how the human lung is inflated by the action of the diaphragm. Use a one-gallon glass jug — with the bottom removed — for the thorax.

3. Draw and color a poster-sized illustration of the human larynx, showing major cartilages and muscles, as well as the vocal folds. Carefully label the parts.

4. Prepare a short oral reading that illustrates the use of a foreign accent or a dialect of English different from the one you normally use.

5. Prepare a poster that displays and explains the major symbols — vowel and consonant — of the International Phonetic Alphabet.

CHAPTER SEVEN

READING THE WRIGHTING

Reading isn't as popular as it once was. Some people blame it on television and movies, saying that these modern forms of communication encourage sitting passively and merely allowing the images to "wash over" you. It's true that reading requires greater effort — both physical and mental — than watching movies or television, but today's students (particularly drama students) aren't as lazy as many of these experts seem to believe!

Lucky thing, too, since reading plays is even *more* demanding than reading stories or novels. Why? Because the author of a story or novel often communicates the mood and meaning of a particular scene by describing the setting in great detail.

> Standing with his back to the window, Claude could feel the heat of the sun through the dense weave of his perfectly pressed charcoal gray jacket. The smell of freshly mown lawns permeated the room, bringing to his mind the lost days of his childhood when everything seemed both mysterious and possible. As he stepped into the shadows, his eyes searching for the shimmer of sunlight on Sheila's satin skin, he knew that his life would be forever changed by the events of this devilishly delightful day.

Pardon the purple prose, but you get the idea. Not only do we know where he's standing and what he's wearing and even the approximate season and time of day, we even know what he's thinking. Novelists have it easy! And, in a way, so do their readers.

In a play, almost all of the information is conveyed through the dialog. Of course there are stage directions, sometimes — at the beginning of the act or scene — including

WHERE DO *STAGE DIRECTIONS* COME FROM?

Those scripts called *Acting Editions*, from publishers such as Samuel French, Inc. and Contemporary Drama Service, often contain very detailed stage directions. You may be surprised to learn that — in most cases — the playwright didn't write these directions. During the Broadway run of a show, the publisher often hires the Stage Manager to provide a detailed set of stage directions from the production. These directions are the result of the designers, director, and cast *of that particular production*, and while they do provide clues to help the reader, experienced actors and directors learn to ignore them when working on a different production of the play!

descriptions of the setting. But except for soliloquies (not too popular in today's theatre), we have only the words that Claude actually speaks to other characters to reveal his thoughts and emotions. Other characters can talk about Claude, contributing to our overall impression of him — but only through the filter of their own perceptions, thoughts, and emotions.

What about Claude's movements and gestures? What about his facial expressions? Don't those show us something about what he's feeling and thinking? Yes, they certainly do, and when we actually *see* a play in production, these clues provide a large part of our information about Claude. But when we *read* a play, most of this information is not given to us — we have to fill in the blanks, use our imaginations to picture the stage setting, the characters' movements and expressions, even their tones of voice.

The ability to hear and see this imaginary production, to transform the written words to sounds and pictures, is the essence of play production. And play production usually begins with somebody writing a script, and somebody else reading it, liking it, and deciding to produce it.

Some Tips on Reading Plays

First of all, make sure you understand the way plays are printed. Generally, three styles of type are used: ALL CAPS (and/or **bold** FACE) for character names, italics for stage directions, and standard for the actual dialog. A typical section of a published play might look like this:

> TOM: (*Standing beside the fireplace as he burns the pages from his book*) I just can't believe I ever thought there was a chance for me to be a successful writer.
>
> MARTHA: Tom, please stop! (*Then to FRED*) Can't you make him stop?

TOM: Stay back, Fred!

FRED: (*Moving toward TOM*) Listen to her, Tom! She's trying to tell you something important.

IF THEY WRITE PLAYS, WHY ARE THEY CALLED PLAYWRIGHTS?

Nowadays, a playwright is about the only person we hear of who is called a *wright*, but it used to be a much more common term. There were shipwrights, wheelwrights, wainwrights, and others. A wright is a builder or maker or constructor, a skilled craftsman who carefully prepares each piece and part of his work, then assembles them into the finished product. If you meet somebody named Wainwright, it's safe to assume that one of his or her ancestors was a wagon maker. It's just a coincidence, but an interesting one, that Wilbur and Orville Wright built bicycles and airplanes. And don't forget the great American architect, Frank Lloyd Wright!

It's important to read the character names, because you need to keep track of who is doing the talking. And it's important to read the dialog — that's what this is all about! The stage directions are less important. If you have a good imagination and a good "silent ear" for dialog (you can almost hear the words in your head as you read them silently), you can probably skip most shorter stage directions without losing anything vital to your understanding of the play. On the other hand, if you suddenly find yourself at sea, unable to understand what's happening in a scene, go back and read it again, this time including the stage directions.

Don't try to read too fast. Dialog is written to be spoken and heard, and it helps if you read silently as if you were hearing the words delivered by actors on a stage. Generally speaking, this means that a play that takes two hours to watch in performance should take about two hours to read.

Don't let the reading go too slowly. If you read only a few pages a day, the two-hour play might take several weeks to complete. That would be like watching a two-hour videotaped movie in three- or four-minute chunks. By the time you get to the beginning of Act II, you'll have forgotten the middle of Act I, and the confusion will lead directly to boredom. Try to read at least an entire act before you take an intermission!

The Elements and Structure of Drama

A cake is made of flour, sugar, eggs, shortening, and other ingredients. What are the main ingredients that, properly mixed, make a play? Most "recipes" would include **plot, theme**, and **character**. Let's take a look at each of these three elements of drama, one at a time.

Most people think of the **plot** of a play as if it were the same as the story of the play. The world is full of plays (and songs, and stories, and novels, and movies) that follow this general plot: boy meets girl; boy loses girl; boy gets girl. A recap of the plot is what you get when you ask the question, "What happens in the play?" The plot is organized around units such as *exposition, inciting incident, crisis, climax,* and *denouement.*

If you ask the question, "What is the play about?" you should expect a different answer: the **theme**. To illustrate the difference between the two questions and the two answers, let's consider a story familiar to almost everybody, "Little Red Riding Hood."

> ***What happens in the story?*** A little girl is sent to deliver food to her grandmother. Although the little girl is cautioned to stay on the path through the forest and avoid strangers, she leaves the path and tells the wolf where she's going and why. When she arrives at her grandmother's house, she is eaten by the wolf — who has already consumed the grandmother.

GENERIC PLOT

We meet the main character (PROTAGONIST), along with other characters, and the EXPOSITION reveals the ANTECEDENT ACTION. The plot starts to move (INCITING INCIDENT) when the protagonist begins trying to achieve a goal or OBJECTIVE. CONFLICT occurs because the protagonist is prevented from easily reaching his/her goal by a series of OBSTACLES, often in the form of a competing character (ANTAGONIST). Each obstacle is confronted in a CRISIS. Finally, the outcome of the protagonist's striving hangs in the balance at the CLIMAX. Finally, the "loose ends" of the story are neatly tied up in the DENOUEMENT.

Why we need EXPOSITION

LIFETIME OF THE MAIN CHARACTERS

Basic Dramatic Structure

What is the story about? It's about the importance of following directions and not talking to strangers.

The obvious difference between the two answers is that the description of the plot is longer. *How much* longer depends on how many details from the original story are included in the answer to the "what happens..." question. A theme should always be expressed in only one sentence.

Every play has at least one **character** — somebody has to perform the action and speak the words! Most often a playwright creates several characters for a play. The characters are carefully constructed to provide contrast and the opportunity for conflict — if the characters were all the same, the play would be extremely boring.

Different kinds of plays combine these ingredients in different proportions. In serious plays, like tragedy or drama, where character development and motivation are important, major characters are given complete, if fictional, biographies; the reader or viewer gets to know these characters both inside and out. In lighter works like farce or melodrama, even the main characters often seem flat or two-dimensional because the plot is more important than the characters or the theme. There are even plays where both plot and character are less important than theme: *Everyman*, the medieval morality play is a good example.

Types and Styles of Plays

It's extremely difficult to study any complicated subject unless it is first divided into smaller, easier to handle ideas. Also, people seem to feel more comfortable discussing things (or even thinking about them) when they have names for them. For these reasons, people have assigned almost every play ever written to one or the other of many categories or genres.

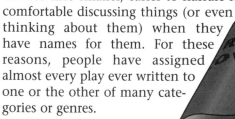

Of course, plays are identified by writer ("one of Shakespeare's plays") and by the time and place in which they were written (Greek, Elizabethan, American, British,

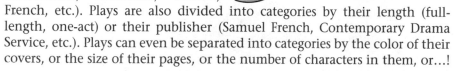

French, etc.). Plays are also divided into categories by their length (full-length, one-act) or their publisher (Samuel French, Contemporary Drama Service, etc.). Plays can even be separated into categories by the color of their covers, or the size of their pages, or the number of characters in them, or...!

Which kinds of categories are better? It depends on what you're trying to do. An interior decorator might be most interested in the color of the cover. A high school drama teacher is apt to be very interested in categorizing by cast size and balance (number of male roles and number of female roles). A drama student who waited too long to get started on a play report might be most interested in the categories *short, shorter*, and *shortest!*

Types of Plays

Tragedy! Comedy! Drama! Melodrama! Farce! Satire! These are just a few of the types of plays. A published play often includes one of these words on the cover as a clue to the reader about the contents of the book *(a comedy in one act,* or *a drama in three acts,* for example). While most people have a general idea of what is meant by most of these terms, a student of theatre needs to take a closer look.

Some plays are serious, others are funny. Some serious plays contain funny scenes or lines, while some funny plays have serious messages or themes. And there are different kinds of "funny." How can we make sense of all this? Many students find it useful to think of types of plays as if they are part of a continuum — a line that stretches, unbroken, from the most serious to the most comedic. This way of looking at it has limitations, but it does provide a convenient starting point.

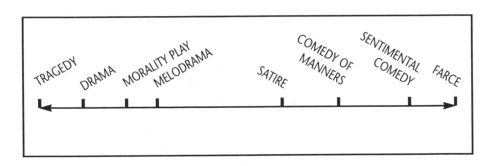

The sample shown above will give you a look at the way the idea works. But how do we decide if a play is a tragedy or a drama, a farce or a sentimental comedy? And exactly how do we decide which type goes where?

Each play can be classified by looking at its characteristics, the same way that foods can be classified by looking at their ingredients: animal or vegetable, grain or legume, high protein or high carbohydrate. Now, before you get too hungry, let's look at some of the major types of plays.

Tragedy is one of the oldest types of drama. It has been with us since the days of the great Greek playwrights Æschylus, Sophocles, and Euripedes. When we hear on the news or read in the papers of a train wreck or plane crash that killed a great many people, we often find the word tragedy used

56

Reading the Wrighting

to describe the situation. In general usage, tragedy means something like *very sad*, but in the study of drama it has a much more specific meaning. Aristotle, the Greek philosopher, gave us the oldest definition of tragedy. His definition includes the following elements:

> The play must be of a serious nature, intended to provide the audience with an emotional catharsis, or cleansing, by arousing deep feelings of horror and pity.

> The play must adhere to the three unities: time, place, and action. That is, the story of the play must take no longer than one day, it must take place in only one location, and it must not be interrupted or diluted by sub-plots.

> The play must feature a tragic hero: a person of exalted state (a king, or a prince, or somebody important in his world), who is essentially a good man but has a tragic flaw in his character such as excessive pride.

> Fate or destiny brings the tragic hero to a crisis point where he is forced to choose between two courses of action, neither of which is obviously better than the other.

> The hero is destroyed by his choice.

Œdipus Rex is an excellent example of Greek tragedy. Some purists maintain that only the Greeks wrote tragedy — and this is true if your definition of tragedy is restricted to the Greek definition! Most people accept a broader definition that includes a wider selection of plays. *Hamlet* and *Othello* are good examples of Shakespearean tragedy. Some people believe that *Death of a Salesman,* by Arthur Miller, is a modern tragedy, even though its hero, Willy Loman, is only an ordinary salesman who has been bypassed by the modern world.

Comedy is a more general term, applied to any play that has a happy ending — even if the play isn't funny. Plays ranging from Shakespeare's *As You Like It* to Oscar Wilde's *Lady Windermere's Fan* to Anton Chekhov's *Uncle Vanya* to Neil Simon's *The Odd Couple* are all comedies.

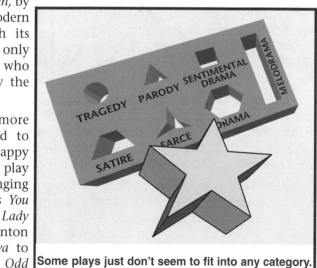

Some plays just don't seem to fit into any category.

57

Even murder mysteries such as Agatha Christie's *The Mousetrap* are, technically, comedies.

Drama is a general category for serious plays about serious subjects. Character development and theme are usually more important than plot. Ibsen's *A Doll's House* is a drama, as is *Miss Julie*, by Strindberg.

Melodrama is the category for plays about serious subjects where plot is more important than character and theme. Characters tend to be rather flat, and they don't change or develop during the course of the play. Murder mysteries and suspense thrillers fit in this category.

Sentimental Drama is the "soap opera" category. Serious subjects are treated in a serious manner; plot and character are more important than theme. There is usually a heavy emphasis on the emotions of the characters. *The Dark at the Top of the Stairs*, by William Inge, is a good example.

Sentimental Comedy is the "sit com," or situation comedy, category. Subjects are usually lighter, and are treated with humor. Major emphasis is on plot and character. Neil Simon's *Barefoot in the Park* fits in this category.

Farce is often called "low comedy." The emphasis is almost entirely on plot, with bawdy jokes and physical humor. Elements of farce include such things as *chases, disguises, talking at cross purposes*, and *slapstick (pratfalls, slipping on banana peels, etc.).* Feydeau's *A Flea in Her Ear* is a farce.

Theater of the Absurd contains elements of many other types. It

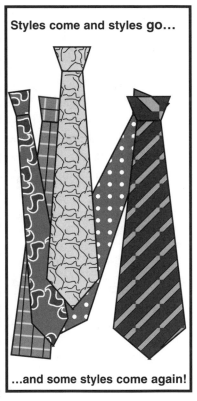

Styles come and styles go...

...and some styles come again!

is usually defined by its underlying theme of the meaningless nature (or *absurdity*) of life. Often, the very structure of the play reinforces this idea, as in Ionesco's *The Bald Soprano* and Beckett's *Waiting for Godot*.

Comedy of Manners is a "high comedy" category. The emphasis is on the cleverness and witty dialog of the characters, who are usually members of the upper class. The great comedies of the English Restoration (1660–1725) and Eighteenth Century (Farquhar's *The Beaux' Stratagem* and Sheridan's *The Rivals*, for example) and Wilde's *The Importance of Being Earnest* fit in this style.

Satire is also considered to be high comedy. In satire, the playwright pokes fun at social customs and current fashions — sometimes including specific individuals of the times — perhaps in an effort to change current thought and behavior. Aristophanes satirized many elements of Greek culture in his plays. Molière's satires, such as *The Imaginary Invalid*, *Tartuffe*, and *The Would-be Gentleman* were sometimes so biting that his career was threatened.

Parody is a specific form of satire in which a very familiar play/song/movie/etc. is recreated in a humorous way, poking fun at the original version.

Musical Comedy is possibly America's only original contribution to dramatic literature. It features spoken dialog combined with songs and dances — and since *Oklahoma!* by Rodgers and Hammerstein, the songs are integrated into the action, a real change from the older *operetta* form (like the works of Rudolph Friml and Sigmund Romberg).

Social Drama is the serious counterpart of satire. Current social problems are examined in a serious manner. Many excellent social dramas were written in America during the 1930s, such as Clifford Odets' *Waiting for Lefty*. Modern serious plays dealing with homelessness, for example, or drug addiction, or child abuse, or teenage violence would fit within this category, if their intent seems to be to change prevailing attitudes and policies.

Styles of Plays

Style is a word with an elusive meaning. Most often it is used as a synonym for *fashion* — either you have it, or you don't! But it's also commonly used in discussions about architecture and interior decorating, as in *early American style* furniture, or the *contemporary style*. Sometimes these styles refer to specific historical periods, as when we talk about the *baroque period* or the *French impressionist period* in painting. Sometimes the styles are more specific: one of the styles of impressionism in painting — made famous by George Seurat, the title character of the musical, *Sunday Afternoon in the Park With George* — was called *pointillism*.

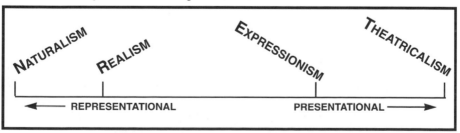

In drama, as in art, architecture, music, clothing, and other areas, styles come and styles go, changing with the changing times. What was once new and fresh becomes old and stale. But some styles seem to have nine lives. Something about them is so strong, or pure, or true that they are rediscovered in a new generation. Elements of one style are often combined with elements of another to create a hybrid style such as *expressionistic realism* (or type, as in *tragi-comedy*).

Naturalism vs. Theatricalism

For years, many people have complained about "modern art" because the paintings "don't look like anything." Most people are accustomed to seeing familiar objects represented in paintings: houses, people, sky, sea, and so on. Defenders of modern art respond by saying things like, "Just look at the painting and accept it for what it is! Don't worry about what it's 'supposed' to be!"

These two opposing views have a place in theatre, too. Again, we can show them at opposite ends of a continuum. Last time we put tragedy at one end and farce at the other. This time, we'll put naturalism at one end and theatricalism at the other end.

Naturalism is the "realer than real" or "slice of life" style. David Belasco, the American producer and director of plays like *The Girl of the Golden West* in the early days of the twentieth century, once purchased a complete diner, had it disassembled and moved to the theatre where it was reassembled — down to the running water and working stoves — on the stage for one of his productions. *The Lower Depths*, by Maxim Gorky, exemplifies naturalism.

Realism is the style most people expect when they go to the theatre, perhaps because that's what they see in the movies. When the curtain rises, they see what looks like "a suburban living room," or "the adjoining backyards of two homes, with the back porches of the two houses in the rear." Or some such. At any rate, the scenery "represents" something — and usually

> **PARADOX 1**
>
> Plays are (almost always) performed on the stage of a theatre. Isn't it strange that when the producers, designers, director and actors have spent many hours and many dollars making the stage and the actors look like something it isn't (a suburban living room, for example, peopled with a struggling writer, her husband, two children, a best friend, and two neighbors), we call it *realism?*

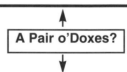

A Pair o'Doxes?

> **PARADOX 2**
>
> Naturalistic plays like *The Lower Depths* are called "slice of life" plays because the characters, setting, and action seem so lifelike in their spontaneity and unplanned effect. But don't forget that the playwright spent a great deal of time *choosing* from all the possible characters and locales and incidents —and then *arranging* them in the manner that best conveys his message. That's what makes it art instead of accident!

something at least slightly familiar. The costumes, props, lighting, and even the acting follow suit. Sherwood Anderson's The *Petrified Forest* is a good example of this style.

Theatricalism is just that: pure theatre, with no attempt to pretend otherwise. Plays that feature such characters as clowns, acrobats, or even actors are almost always very theatrical. They make no pretense of being anything other than a play. The setting of the play is often plainly revealed as the stage of a theatre. Full of speeches directed out to the audience (sometimes in the actor's "voice" rather than the character's) — plays such as Thornton Wilder's *The Skin of Our Teeth* seek to *present* the idea of the play to the audience rather than *represent* something else. Many plays contain elements of theatricalism.

Expressionism uses theatrical techniques, often including exaggerated colors and shapes in the scenery, to reveal the emotions of the characters — usually as they relate to the stresses and anxieties caused by the depersonalization of life in modern industrialized society. Elmer Rice's *The Adding Machine* is an excellent example of theatrical expressionism.

Classicism or **Neo-classicism** is a style that consciously imitates the Greek or Roman classics. These plays adhere to the three unities or otherwise imitate the perceived virtues of classic drama. Racine's *Phedre* is a neo-classic play.

Romanticism is often full of strong emotion, and often projects the idea of the perfectibility of mankind or a yearning for the simpler days of the past. It's generally optimistic and hopeful. Rostand's *Cyrano de Bergerac* is a familiar romantic play.

A Final Caution

Two important things to remember about types and styles of plays are that most plays combine elements from more than one type or style, and there are many more types and styles than those listed in this chapter. These categories are created and applied *after* the plays have been written. They are useful as guidelines for evaluating and comparing plays, but they are *only* guidelines, not hard and fast rules!

Exercises:

1. Perform (with a partner) a rehearsed improvisation to demonstrate one of the types or styles of plays discussed in this chapter.

2. Write a 10- to 15-minute scene illustrating one of the styles or types of plays discussed in this chapter.

3. Read a play (full-length or one-act) and prepare a report in which you explain to the class — specifically, using details from the play — what the style/type of the play is and what the plot and theme are.

4. Paint or draw a poster depicting a scene from a play in one of the recognized styles of art (romanticism, impressionism, cubism, expressionism, etc.). Explain your choice of style to the class.

5. Read a full-length play and prepare a poster-sized chart showing the structure of the play, listing specific events from the script that fulfill the requirements of *inciting incident, crisis, climax,* etc. from the diagram on page 54. Explain your chart to the class.

CHAPTER EIGHT

MEETING THE MONOLOG

Sooner or later, every student of acting must come to grips with preparing and performing a monolog, whether it's an audition for a specific role, or for a place in a repertory company, or simply a course requirement (like this). Although the specifics of length and scene selection may vary from one set of circumstances to another, the process of getting a monolog ready for performance is much the same in all cases.

What is a monolog? Basically, it's the singular version of a dialog: one character, alone on-stage, speaking to himself, or to the audience, or to an invisible other character.

Finding Monologs

Where does an actor find a monolog? Basically, there are three sources of monologs. Let's take a look at each source.

Write–It–Yourself Monologs

If you're preparing an audition for a regional repertory company, or for a scholarship to a drama school, you may want to write your own material. After all, you know your own strengths and weaknesses better than anyone else, and you can write a monolog to showcase your best points. Be sure, though, that you have carefully read any rules or guidelines for the audition. Many such rules, in fact almost all of them, will specify the source of your material, and few of them allow the use of other than published material.

Special Monolog Books

There is a growing body of material available which has been written and published specifically for use as audition monologs. These have the advantage of being "fresher" than the same tired old scenes from famous plays, but be sure that the audition guidelines allow this kind of material.

Published Plays

The most common source of monologs is plays that have proven themselves by being performed widely and published by a reputable publisher. Many books of scenes and monologs taken from these plays are available, and many of them are specifically devoted to certain categories of plays (Acting Scenes From the Classics, Monologues From New American Plays, etc.).

Experienced actors, or those who have seen or read a substantial number of plays, often do their own "cutting" of monologs from scripts. Monologs cut from plays come from four different types of scenes. Some plays have lengthy sections in which one character directly addresses the audience (the Stage Manager's opening speech in *Our Town,* by Thornton Wilder, for example). Others contain scenes with long speeches directed to another character (or characters) on the stage (Elizabeth's speech to Essex in the last act of *Elizabeth the Queen,* by Maxwell Anderson, is a good example). Still other plays, primarily the classics, contain long speeches in which the character addresses either himself or nobody in particular (almost any play by Shakespeare contains several such soliloquies). Finally, some plays contain scenes between two or more characters which can be cut and slightly rewritten so that one of the characters can carry the scene, pausing to listen to the "other" character, sometimes taking the other character's lines for his or her own, sometimes filling in the gaps with bits of new dialog added for the purpose (the soda fountain scene between George Gibbs and Emily Webb from *Our Town* can be done as a monolog for either character).

Choosing a Monolog

Finding material that's just right — for you and for the intended audience — can be just as rewarding as the search for it can be frustrating. As beginners, though, it's easy to allow the search for the perfect monolog to become an excuse for not getting to work preparing any monolog. Take a look at the monologs suggested by your teacher, and pick the one you like best — or flip a coin! You'll learn more about acting by actually rehearsing than by debating the relative merits of various monologs.

> # Confucius says:
> ## *The longest journey begins with a single step.*
>
> ---
>
> # Lee says:
> ## *Yes, but it doesn't end there!*

If you know of a monolog other than those suggested by the teacher, please keep this in mind when you make your selection: for your first effort choose a scene in which the focus is kept on-stage. That is, don't do a monolog in which your character speaks directly to the audience. This will force you to work on creating a stage reality — and keep you from having to look into the eyes of the audience.

Because we are not preparing an audition piece, it is quite acceptable, maybe even preferable, to choose a character who is quite a bit different from you. In the real world of acting, you won't get the opportunity to play characters very different from yourself, so take advantage of this chance to try your hand at some of the great parts from the great plays, like Willy Loman from *Death of a Salesman*, or Cyrano, or Joan of Arc, or Elizabeth I, or . . . well, you get the idea.

A Word About Length

"How long does it have to be?" is the question most hated by drama teachers everywhere, because it shows that the student's mind is focusing on the wrong things. Try not to let the length of a piece be the sole criterion you use in the selection process. For a class assignment, anything between two-and-a-half and five minutes long is suitable. Sometimes an even shorter monolog is okay, particularly if it has special problems like unusual language or a difficult dialect.

The Rehearsal Process

Don't be overwhelmed by the thought of having to prepare and perform a monolog for the first time. Take your time to work through the following steps, one step at a time, and you'll find that the job is much less daunting than you feared.

> Ω
>
> **Sitting down and reading through the script (more than once or twice), is like learning to swim by sitting near the pool and thinking about it. You may not *drown* when you finally get into the water for the competition, but it will most certainly be a strange and uncomfortable feeling!**
>
> Ω

1. Read through the script to make sure you understand the meaning and pronunciation of all the words. A good dictionary will supply most of the missing knowledge.

2. Understand what's happening in the scene. If possible, read the entire play from which the scene has been cut. At the very least, read the notes about the play which usually accompany the cutting.

3. Use a pencil and paper to design a simple set. Determine the location of doors, windows, and furniture. Include all those objects you will use or specifically refer to in the scene. Even though your set will be composed

of nothing more elaborate than a few chairs and possibly a table or two, it's important for you to know exactly what items they represent, and to know the general layout of the entire room — including those items not used or referred to in the scene. Be specific: it helps both you and the audience believe in the reality you're creating on-stage. Be consistent: once you've laid out the floor plan (and perhaps revised it after the first couple of rehearsals) use the same plan at all rehearsals. It will mean one less thing for you to have to think about when you actually perform.

4. Plan the *blocking* for the scene. The blocking is the movement around the stage (XDR, XC above table, sit in DL chair, etc.). Some movements are clearly indicated by the script (although you needn't feel obligated to use all or any of the stage directions from the published material). Other movements will occur to you as you work through the scene, as ways to make the character's inner life visible to the audience.

5. Walk through the scene with your script and a pencil. Say all the lines and perform all the blocking you've planned. The pencil is for making changes in the blocking, or marking special points of emphasis in the script.

6. Repeat step 5. Then repeat it again. And again. After four or five walk-throughs, the set and blocking will have resolved themselves into their (more or less) final shapes. Make sure that you have included in your "vision" of the scene the location(s) of the other character(s) on the stage. It's helpful to establish a specific location, such as sitting in the chair next to the table, for another character. Anchoring him or her to a single place makes it easy for you to keep track of the focus of your lines, and helps the audience "see" the other character, too.

7. By this time, you are probably finding that the script and pencil are getting in your way, preventing you from doing bits of character business (such as pulling at your ear, or writing notes, or adjusting your clothing, or anything else that shows what your character is like). For the next few run-throughs, work on getting your eyes off the page while you're speaking. Look down at the script, putting the next phrase or sentence into your short-term memory, then look up from the script as you speak the words. Doing this several times paves the way for memorization without worry.

8. Memorization is *the* bugaboo for most beginning actors. It doesn't need to be a big problem, especially if you have followed the previous steps, but it is something that must happen — it's as basic to acting as tying your shoes is to playing basketball. You'll probably be pleasantly surprised to discover that you have already "memorized" a pretty fair amount of the scene in your repeated walk-throughs with eyes off the page, but there comes a time when you must leave the script in your pocket or somewhere outside your setting. I know that it feels terrible, and that all the fun and flow of

the scene vanish as you grope for your next words. The thing is, this awful feeling is going to happen no matter how long you wait to put down the script, so it's better to do it as early as possible in the preparation process. That way you get over the "off-book blues" in plenty of time to apply the finishing touches to your characterization.

Try to find somebody to hold the script and follow it as you say the lines; if you absolutely can't remember what comes next, say "Line," and he or she can read you enough to get you going again. If no prompter is available, you'll need to set the script aside, then begin your rehearsal. When you can't think of the next line, stay calm and in character while you check the script, then return it to its place before continuing the rehearsal.

9. Take the time to write a brief introduction for your monolog. Include your name, the name of the character you're playing, the title of the play the cutting is taken from, and the playwright's name. Optional information — included as it seems necessary to help the audience understand what they're about to see — could include a brief description of the setting ("There is a large window stage right, and a fireplace stage left.") and/or a brief summary of previous action in the play that leads up to your scene. Practice saying the introduction several times until it sounds prepared and polished.

Performing the Monolog

When it's your turn to perform, you should walk quietly to the stage, quickly arrange the furniture to fit your needs, then step to down center and begin your introduction.

At the end of your introduction, quietly move to your position at the beginning of the monolog. Pause long enough for a couple of deep breaths, giving yourself a chance to get into character, then begin the monolog.

When you have said the last line, pause for a moment to allow the character to be replaced by your own personality. And there may be applause! Then resume your seat.

Evaluating the Performance

While specific evaluation or grading criteria will vary from school to school and teacher to teacher, some expectations are pretty much the same no matter where you are. The following hints and tips should help you get the best possible grade for your monolog.

Never apologize for your work! Part of an actor's task is to make the audience feel safe — to keep them from being afraid for the actor, afraid that they'll have to feel embarassed for the actor. Everything you do and say should be planned to build the impression that you know exactly what you're doing and that the audience is going to enjoy your performance. The way you walk to the stage, the way you set the stage, your introduction — all these should exude confidence and control. Above all, never say anything like "This probably won't be very good," or "I'm not really ready."

Remember that memorization is important, but rehearsal is even more important. By the time you perform your monolog, you should have rehearsed so many times that your level of preparation will carry you through the inevitable stage fright which will otherwise drive every line and every piece of character business from your head.

Stay in character. Even if you do have a brief lapse of memory, the audience won't know it as long as you don't give it away by breaking character — giggling, making eye contact with the audience, correcting or berating yourself out loud ("I knew it before," or "Wait a minute, I should have said . . ."). And if you really run into a blank wall and can't remember what comes next, stay cool and cut to the next part of the scene that you can remember. The audience doesn't know the script, and they'll probably never notice that you left out a few words.

Exercises:

Select, prepare, rehearse and perform a monolog. Follow the steps as given in this chapter. *Take full advantage of class time given for rehearsal.* If you need extra help, arrange with your teacher to come in for extra coaching.

CHAPTER NINE

FAMILY ALBUM, PART II:
MEDIEVAL AND RENAISSANCE THEATRE

Roman Theatre

Following the Golden Age of Greek drama, the Roman Empire ruled throughout the Mediterranean area. Theatre flourished during Roman times, and many theatres were built throughout the empire. These theatres largely followed the Greek tradition of semicircular seating areas and round or half-round orchestras with the stage behind, but the Romans built their versions as freestanding buildings instead of carving them from a hillside.

Roman drama and theatre are represented in our family album by the plays of Plautus and Terence, both of whom wrote before Rome had any permanent theatres. **Plautus** wrote comedies, perhaps building on the New Comedy traditions of Menander and other Greeks. His plays, of which twenty survive, often featured complicated plots with disguises, mistaken identities, and other farcical elements. Shakespeare borrowed from Plautus' *The Menæchmi* when he wrote *Two Gentlemen of Verona*.

Terence lived and wrote after Plautus' death. Only a few of his plays survive, but they indicate that he wrote in a more refined style, with less of the ribald buffoonery of Plautus. *Phormio* is occasionally performed even today.

Most Roman tragic playwrights contented themselves with adapting and reworking the Greek tragedies. **Seneca**, the chief Roman writer of tragedies, was the only significant writer from the time when Rome had permanent theatres. His tragedies were evidently not intended for public performance, but rather for private reading. (The reason they are often called closet tragedies is that a person's private room used to be called a closet; it has nothing to do with the commonly held opinion that the closet is the best place for them!)

Literary drama was not the only expression of the theatrical impulse during Roman times. Following another tradition from Greece, a Roman popular theatre flourished in marketplaces and public squares. Small portable stages were used for the presentation of popular farces and satires. These plays used and developed *stock characters* such as the braggart soldier, the clever servant, the foolish old man, and the young lovers. The structure

69

of these plays and interplay of their characters have proven to be one of the most durable of theatrical traditions, leading to the *commedia dell'arte* of the Renaissance and beyond.

The designation of Christianity as the official religion of the Roman Empire effectively put an end to theatrical endeavors. The church frowned on theatre as a frivolous — if not downright sinful — activity. With the sacking of Rome and the end of the Empire in the fourth century, literary drama, along with almost all intellectual, artistic and cultural activities, came to an end.

> **STOCK CHARACTERS are those who remain the same in many different plays. Each one is easy to recognize because of his or her name, typical costume, and obvious personality traits.**

Medieval Theatre

The medieval period was a time of intellectual and cultural stagnation and darkness (hence the name, Dark Ages). Without the unifying political and cultural force of Rome, and its extensive network of well-maintained roads, transportation and communication became difficult. Small areas became isolated and independent of each other, and the feudal system (many serfs living on and working the land of a powerful ruler, in return for his protection from raiders) became the prevalent form of political organization or government.

The Catholic church quickly became the primary unifying force. Its bishops and priests were trained and controlled by the central hierarchy. They exercised great power over the people, at least partly because only those in the church could read the Bible (or anything else, for that matter). This meant that for most Europeans during the medieval period, the only path to salvation lay in following the dictates of the church.

It is ironic that the church — which had ended theatre in late Roman times — was responsible for the rebirth of theatre in the late medieval period. Sometime around the ninth century, the church began using elements of drama and theatre as additions to its celebration of the Mass. These small playlets were called *tropes*, and were probably developed in order to make it easier for the congregation to learn and appreciate the message of the church.

The first one may have been the *Quæm queritas trope*, used during the Easter season. Instead of simply having the priest tell the story of the three Marys finding the tomb empty on Easter morning, the scene was acted out. Three priests, deacons, or acolytes pretended to be the three women, and

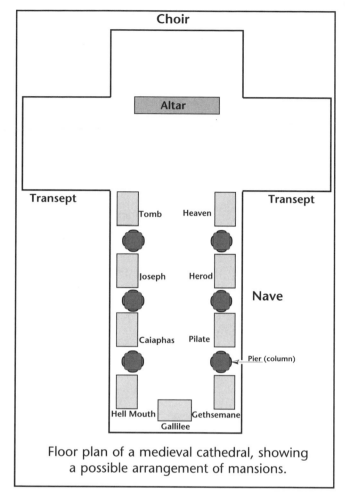

Floor plan of a medieval cathedral, showing
a possible arrangement of mansions.

another pretended to be the angel they discover in the tomb. When the "women" approach the tomb and discover that the stone has been removed, the angel asks them, "Quæm queritas? (Whom seek ye here?)"

This simple theatrical experiment proved to be so effective and so popular that more scenes were soon acted out. Separate areas of the church were used for each scene, with small stages, called *mansions*, set up for each one. The area between and around the mansions was called the *plain* and could be used for scenes taking place on a road, in the desert, or in other undifferentiated locales.

Three distinct types of liturgical plays were developed: *mystery plays* (stories from the Bible), *miracle plays* (stories of the saints), and *morality plays* (allegories, with characters representing abstract values, that taught right from wrong). All three stressed the didactic or instructional value of theatre.

71

The responsibility for each mansion was assumed by a medieval *guild* — something like a modern labor union or trade organization. The bakers' guild, for example, might take charge of Hells' Mouth because they were accustomed to working in heat and smoke, while the fishermen's guild might produce the story of Jonah and the whale.

The plays increased in popularity as their creators grew more inventive in building mansions and acting out the plays. As popularity grew, the plays were moved out of the churches and into the public squares. In England, the mansions became wheeled *pageant wagons*, and the Cycle Plays of Wakefield and York, for example, could be performed over wide areas with the audience remaining in one place while the various scenes were moved around them.

The *passion play* also evolved during this period. This kind of play depicts scenes from the life of Christ. These have remained popular to the present day. The oldest still-active, over three hundred years old, is performed at Oberammergau, a small Bavarian village, every ten years.

The church became disenchanted with the plays, partly because of the humorous depictions of Herod, Satan, and other biblical villains, and disassociated itself from the productions. This completes the irony mentioned earlier: the church reinvented theatre for its own use, then withdrew its support when theatre once again became secular and popular.

The Second Shepherd's Play (one of the cycle plays) and *Everyman* (a morality play) are among those still available for reading and production. A few secular (nonreligious) plays were written and performed during the late medieval period. Scripts for *Gammer Gurton's Needle* and *Master Pierre Patelin* have survived, and prove very popular when performed today.

The Renaissance in Italy and Spain

The medieval period was ended by a rebirth of learning and cultural activity. Beginning in the late fourteenth or early fifteenth century, the *Renaissance* spread northward from the Mediterranean Sea. It was an exciting time, and many famous artists and scholars flourished: Botticelli, Leonardo da Vinci, and Michelangelo, to name only a few.

In Italy, theatre developed along two lines: the popular *commedia dell'arte* and the courtly drama of the Medicis and other wealthy members of the nobility. Each filled an important part of the people's need for theatre.

The *commedia*, probably a descendant of the Roman street theatre, was performed by traveling troupes, including the first female performers in European theatre. A troupe typically consisted of seven men and three women. Each performer had his or her own character, and parts were passed down from parents to children. The stock characters included *Arlecchino* (the clever servant whose costume of patches developed into the diamond designs of the modern Harlequin), *Pantalone* (the foolish old man or father, whose baggy trousers gave us the word pantaloons), *Pedrolino* (Pierrot, lovelorn and moody), and *Columbina* (Columbine, flirtatious and pretty).

The actors improvised each performance. A *scenario*, or plot outline, was posted off-stage, and the cast improvised dialog, songs, and dances. Actually, some of the songs and dances — and even certain bits of dialogue — were probably used over and over again. We do know that actors developed bits of comic business, called *lazzi*, which were considered the property of the performer who created them. These comic performances were extremely popular, and later influenced the writing of the great French playwright, Molière.

In contrast to this theatre-for-the-masses was the courtly drama of the nobility. Wealthy families built ornate private theatres on their estates, and plays were performed on permanent stages with proscenium arches. The first permanent indoor theatre was the *Teatro Farnese,* built in Parma in 1618.

It's interesting that this period of exploding creativity left us with no surviving scripts. The plays were called neoclassic because they imitated the classic style of the plays of ancient Rome and Athens. Their lack of longevity may in part be attributed to the growth of the Italian opera, which attracted a great following among theatre practitioners as well as the general theatre-going public.

During this same period, Spain became interested in theatre. From about 1550 to 1680, Spanish theatre grew and flourished. Its plays and staging were influenced by both the *commedia* and the court plays of Italy.

Three major playwrights filled the theatres. *Cervantes* (1574–1616) is better known today for his great novel, *Don Quijote de la Mancha* (the basis for the successful American musical, *Man of La Mancha*) than for his thirty plays. *Lope de Vega* (1562–1635) wrote a phenomenal total of two thousand plays, many of them filled with beautiful poetry, romance, and action. He also combined comedy with tragedy and produced the first social drama, *Fuente Ovejuna (The Sheep Well)*. The last of the three great playwrights was *Calderón* (1600–1681), who created over two hundred plays noted for their spiritual emphasis and elevated poetry. We still admire his *La vida es sueño (Life Is a Dream)* and *El gran teatro del mundo (The Great World Theatre)*.

Spanish theatre was staged first in open courtyards. Later, theatres were built which resembled those of Elizabethan England, with a roof above the stage and above the galleries where patrons sat. Even those *groundlings* who stood in the area surrounding the stage were protected by an awning in a theatre built in Madrid in 1574. Over forty theatres existed in Madrid when Spain's Golden Age of Theatre ended with the death of Calderón.

In some ways Spanish theatre was more progressive than that of other countries. For example, Spain welcomed actresses to its stage long before

England did, and Spanish actresses were very popular. One of the best, called "La Calderona," became a mistress of King Phillip IV, and later retired to become the Abbess of a convent.

The Spaniards made a great contribution to world theatre. Further evidence of this is the two great characters, created by Spanish authors, who later became famous in other countries. Guillén de Castro wrote a play about the Spanish medieval hero El Cid, which the French playwright Pierre Corneille turned into the famous play, *Le Cid*. Tirso de Molina, another Spanish playwright, was the creator of Don Juan, a character later written about and copied in France, England, and Italy.

Exercises:

1. As a class, read *Everyman* aloud. Discuss elements of the play which reveal aspects of medieval life, as well as the nature of allegory and didactic theatre.

2. Write a plot outline for a morality play. Name and describe each character, then list the sequence of events.

3. Draw/paint a poster, or build a model, of a pageant wagon.

4. Write a report on the Oberammergau Passion play, or another large-scale passion play (such as the one at Eureka Springs, Arkansas or Spearfish, South Dakota in the Black Hills). Include information about production preparations and performance techniques.

5. Draw/paint a poster illustrating at least four of the commedia characters in their traditional costumes.

6. Enact a puppet show along the lines of the *commedia.*

7. Read one of the plays of Lope de Vega or Calderón and report to the class.

CHAPTER TEN
STAGE LIGHTING

For most of theatre's history, lighting the stage consisted only of waiting for the dawn. From the earliest plays of Egypt and Greece, through the glorious plays of Shakespeare and beyond, plays were performed in the open air, lit by the sun.

Torches and candles brought light to the earliest indoor stages. Gaslights were introduced during the middle of the nineteenth century, and later improved by jetting the flame against a piece of limestone (that's why we still sometimes talk about being in the limelight). Open flames caused several famous theatre fires, and the invention of the electric light was welcomed as the herald of a new age of safety.

Advances in lamp and spotlight design have been rapid in the last several decades. It's common now to see lasers in rock concerts, and even musical comedies sometimes use them. But for lighting the stage for a play performance, the basic ideas haven't changed much in the last fifty years.

The Four Functions of Stage Lighting

What is the purpose of stage lighting? What does the lighting designer try to accomplish?

First and foremost, the designer must provide *visibility*. The audience must be able to see the play — otherwise it might as well be radio! In many theatres, where lack of money means a severe shortage of lighting equipment, visibility becomes the only function of stage lighting — and when you think of what Sophocles and Shakespeare accomplished, that's not necessarily a disaster.

The second function of stage lighting is *plausibility*. Modern audiences who attend a realistic production expect to be able to believe that the light on the stage comes from a source within the world of the play. That chandelier, for example, or the lamp on the table, or the fire in the fireplace, or the sun shining through the window. This kind of believability is important in the "willing suspension of disbelief."

Composition is important, too. The lighting designer can paint the stage with light so that some areas are emphasized while others seem less important. This helps the director and the cast convey the right message to the audience.

The last function of stage lighting is *mood*. The lighting designer is responsible for establishing the appropriate mood or tone for the play, and for each scene. As the curtain rises and the lights fade in for the first act, the audience should be able to tell whether the play is a comedy or a drama, whether it is romantic or farcical or tragic.

The Four Properties of Light

Just as the actor can change the pitch, strength, rate, and quality of his or her voice, the designer can change the intensity, color, distribution, and movement of the light on the stage. In each case the purpose is the same: to create the right effect on the audience.

Intensity can be controlled in several ways. The amount of light on a given scene will be decreased if fewer lights are used, if the lights are moved farther away from the scene, if a colored (or even a neutral) filter is put in front of the light, or if a dimmer is used to reduce the amount of electricity flowing through the lamps.

Color is controlled by making the light pass through filters. These filters can be glass (especially in footlights or striplights), or coatings applied directly to the lamps (Christmas-tree lights, for example), gelatin (that's why the word *gels* is often used to refer to any flat color medium used with a spotlight or flood) or plastic. Color changes also occur when a dimmer is used to reduce the intensity of light: the filament of a traditional incandescent lamp (like the ones in table lamps in your home) becomes redder as the light is dimmed.

Distribution is controlled by changing the direction and the shape of the beams of light shining on the stage. If all the light comes from directly overhead, the effect is quite different from a scene in which the light comes from the front or the side. The choice of lighting instruments (floods, strips, Fresnels, Lekos) changes the distribution, too. Each type has its own characteristic beam-spread, and some allow the designer to determine the actual shape of the beam.

Movement is the last of the four properties of light. If the design calls for a change in intensity, color, or distribution during the performance, movement occurs. A slow fade-out is an example of movement. So is the moving beam or changing color of a follow-spot.

Color in Lights

Most of us are familiar with the traditional color wheel. We know that mixing complementary colors (those opposite each other on the color wheel) is supposed to make black. And that mixing two primary colors together (like red and yellow) makes a secondary color (like orange). Why does this happen? How do we see color?

76

Color is a product of light. Light can be thought of as a wave — sort of like a wave at the beach, only much shorter and traveling much faster. Each color of light is a different wavelength; red is the longest and violet is the shortest. White light is composed of a mixture containing all the wavelengths of light that the human eye can see. A prism can be used to separate the wavelengths of white light into individual colors. The same phenomenon accounts for the colorful rainbow in the sky after a rain shower: the tiny water particles in the air act as prisms.

When white light strikes a colored surface, all of the wavelengths are absorbed except the wavelength of the color of the surface. That is, when sunlight (the whitest light) strikes a red shirt, the red wavelength is reflected from the shirt while all the others are absorbed by it. That's why the shirt looks red.

Dyes and paints and inks and pigments — any such material that can be applied to a surface (including the fiber surfaces of threads and yarns), will absorb parts of white light and reflect other parts, according to the color of the pigment. A white shirt reflects all of the wavelengths, while a black shirt reflects none of them.

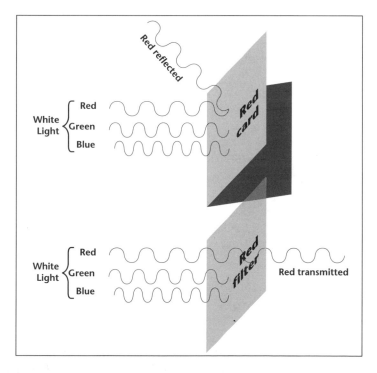

That's why mixing a red paint (absorbs all but the red) and a blue paint (absorbs all but the blue) gives us violet. When all those wavelengths are absorbed — subtracted from the light being reflected — what's left is the wavelength we call violet! And that's why we can create any color by mixing the correct amounts of the *three primary colors of pigment*: red, yellow, and blue. And, since green, a secondary color, is "made up" of equal parts blue and yellow, mixing green and red makes a pigment that absorbs all (or almost all) the wavelengths. The same thing happens when any two complementary colors are mixed. A mixture like this would be black if the primary colors were absolutely pure. In practice, such a mixture results in a very dark gray or brownish–gray.

But that's not the end of the story. In the theatre, mixing pigments is usually the job of the scene designer/painter and the makeup artist. The lighting designer must also know about mixing different colors of light.

Remember, combining all the colors of pigment makes black, but white light is made up of all the wavelengths that the human eye can see. The common method of creating colored light is using a filter, usually a piece of colored plastic, placed between a white light and the surface on which it shines. Such a filter does its job by absorbing all the wavelengths from the white light except the ones that give the light its color–name. That is, a red filter placed in front of a white light absorbs all the wavelengths except red, which is transmitted, or allowed to pass through. Combining the primary colors of light — by shining one light of each color onto a white surface, thus adding together the different wavelengths — results in (surprise, surprise!) white light.

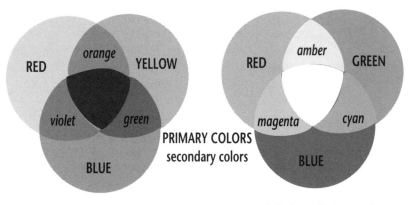

Mixing pigment colors   **Mixing light colors**

The *primary colors of light* differ from those of pigment. Red, green and blue are the primary colors in light. Red light combined with green light produces amber as a secondary color. Red and blue produce magenta, and green and blue produce cyan. Mixing complementary colors of light (red and cyan, for example), produces white light.

What happens when a colored light shines on a colored surface? A beautiful pink ball gown for a romantic play can look muddy and gray if the wrong color of light is chosen by the lighting designer. Which color wheel do we need to use to determine what the effect will be?

Think for a minute about how we see colors on surfaces: a red surface absorbs most of the light wavelengths, reflecting only that part of the spectrum that we call red. But if we put a green filter in front of the light, it absorbs all the light except the green. If we shine this light on the red surface, there is no red light for the surface to reflect, so it will appear black or gray or dark brown. This means that a lighting designer can use the pigment color wheel to determine the effect of colored light shining on a colored surface.

The lighting designer must work closely with the other designers on a show (sets, costumes, makeup). The colors chosen for the set and costumes and makeup will be affected by the colors chosen by the lighting designer, and we want the effects to be the right ones, the ones that contribute positively to the total effect of the performance.

Basic Electricity

Knowing a little bit about electricity is important for anybody who works with stage lighting. It can also come in handy around the house (you won't always live with your parents!). Understanding what happened when the power went off in the kitchen and knowing how to fix it — and how to keep it from happening again — are useful skills. So is being able to replace a worn-out light switch or lamp socket — without damage to yourself or your home.

We are all familiar with electricity because we use it every day. Not many of us know how it works and how to deal safely with it, and nobody — not even a physicist — knows exactly why it works the way it does.

It's probably easiest to understand how electricity works invisibly by comparing it to something visible. In many ways, water flowing through a hose is like electricity flowing through a wire, and using this analogy will make it easier to understand some of the basic concepts and terms of electricity.

Imagine a garden hose with water flowing through it. How many different ways can we measure something about the water?

If you hold your hand in the stream of water as it leaves the hose, you will feel the pressure or force of the water against your hand. Turning the faucet counter-clockwise will increase the amount of pressure. Electricity has a pressure or force, too. It's called *voltage* or *electromotive force*, and it's mea-

79

sured in volts. That's the difference between a 9-volt battery and a 1.5-volt battery, or between a 120-volt electrical outlet (for lamps, televisions, computers, refrigerators, etc.) and a 220-volt outlet (for electric stoves and clothes dryers).

We can also measure the quantity of water flowing through the hose. We might measure it in gallons (or ounces or pounds or liters or kilograms) per minute. The quantity of electricity, or the intensity of its current, is measured in *amperes* (*amps*, for short).

The flow of water through the hose can be restricted by using a nozzle, or putting your thumb over the end of the hose, or putting a kink into the hose, or even by using a narrower hose — anything that will provide *resistance* to the water's flow. The flow of electricity can also be restricted. Electrical resistance is measured in *ohms*. Using a longer wire will restrict the flow of electricity, but putting a kink in the wire won't do it. And for heaven's sake don't try putting your thumb over the end of the wire! Every light bulb, toaster, stereo, or video screen creates resistance.

If we put a nozzle (resistance) on the hose to create pressure against a water wheel or turbine, we can use the flow to perform work. (Maybe not much work, but — on a larger scale — flour mills used to be operated by the flow of a river, and hydroelectric plants use water power to turn their generators.) Electricity has *power*, too. It's measured in *watts*. This measurement is commonly used to tell the difference between light bulbs, for example, and stereo speakers and amplifiers.

GAUGING THE WIRE

Cables and extension cords can get to be very long in the theater — or at home. The longer the cord, the greater the resistance per diameter, so thicker wires are required for longer distances. Larger quantities (amps) of electricity need fatter wires, too. Wire is sold in different thicknesses or gauges. Common lamp cord is only 18 gauge. Thicker wire has smaller gauge numbers, so 14 gauge is thicker than 18, and 12 gauge is even thicker. Be sure to use the right gauge to avoid overloads and possible fires!

GAUGE	AMPS
18	5
16	10
14	15
12	20
10	30

Relationships

Simple observation reveals that restricting the flow of water by partially covering the end of the hose has an effect on the force with which the water leaves the hose. It also has an effect on the quantity of water reaching the ground.

Similar relationships exist between and among volts, amps, ohms, and watts. It's impossible to change the amperage in an electrical circuit without changing either the resistance or the voltage or both. Similarly, changing the wattage in a circuit causes changes in one or more of the other areas. Fortunately, the changes are predictable, following a strict rule that can be applied in advance so that the results will not come as a surprise to the electrician — or the lighting technician.

The exact relationship between electrical measurements was discovered by Monsieur Ohm, whose name was also given to the measurement of electrical resistance. *Ohm's Law* defines the specific relationships between electromotive force, intensity of current, and resistance: **E = IR** (electromotive force equals intensity of current multiplied by resistance). Now, we could use algebra to solve this equation for each of the vari-

A *circuit* has more in common with a *circle* than a *circus* — although there is unquestionably a circus circuit. Electricity flows along a path that starts at the power source (battery, electrical outlet, etc.) and ends back at the power source (the other end of the battery, the other slot of the outlet). It performs work on lamps or bells or motors installed in the circuit. Switches "open" the circuit, breaking the flow of electricity, in order to turn the lamp off.

Electricity will also flow to "ground" — as lightning strikes trees, buildings, and people — so don't put yourself into the circuit!

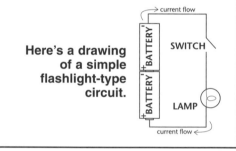

Here's a drawing of a simple flashlight-type circuit.

ables, but (thank goodness!) there is an easier way.

If you can draw a triangle, you can work with Ohm's Law! Here's an example of the kind of triangle you need:

Using a triangle like this makes it easy to solve Ohm's Law problems. The triangle places the three variables, electromotive force, intensity of current, and resistance, into a visual representation of the correct mathematical relationship. The quantity at the top of the triangle is the product of the two at the bottom; either bottom quantity is the result of dividing the top quan-

81

tity by the other bottom quantity. Here's an example of a triangle with actual numbers that shows how it works:

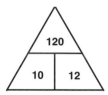

As you can see, 10 x 12 = 120. And 120 ÷ 10 = 12. And it works the other way, too: 120 ÷ 12 = 10! If the 10 is changed to a 5, and the 120 is left the same, the 12 must change to 24 in order to keep the relationships the same (120 ÷ 5 = 24).

Now all you need to add to your memory bank is the unit of measure that goes into each part of the triangle:

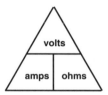

Combining everything we've done so far means that 10 amps multiplied by 12 ohms equals 120 volts.

When you come right down to it, most lighting technicians and designers can go a very long time without having to deal with Ohm's Law, but no self-respecting member of the "juice crew" would admit to not knowing it. More often than not, lighting technicians and designers have to deal with the wattage of various spotlights and matching them to a dimmer circuit for control. Being able to figure out how many spotlights can be controlled by a particular dimmer — without overloading it — is a very handy skill.

Problems like this use something called the *PIE formula*. You can probably guess what it stands for, especially if it's written P = IE, and you'll know not to head for the kitchen! Remember that P stands for *power* (measured in *watts*). The PIE formula tells us that power is equal to intensity of current multiplied by electromotive force (watts equals amps times volts). This means that a 60-watt bulb, used in a standard 120-volt household electrical circuit, requires a flow of .5 amps of electricity (60 ÷ 120 = .5).

And the best news is that the triangle works for the PIE formula just as it does for Ohm's Law:

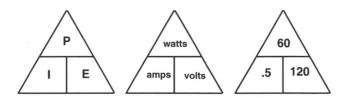

Of course the arithmetic isn't always so simple. Not many spotlights use a 60-watt lamp (what we call a bulb at home is called a lamp in the theatre). A typical spotlight in a small theatre uses a 500-watt lamp. That gives us a triangle like this:

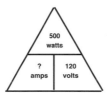

A quick check with a calculator (or even a pencil and paper) shows that 500 ÷ 120 = 4.167. So we know that a 500-watt spotlight, used in a 120-volt circuit, requires 4.167 amps of electricity.

It's a short step from there to being able to figure out how many lights can be controlled by a dimmer in a 120-volt, 20-amp circuit — and this is the bread and butter of the lighting technician.

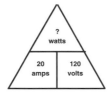
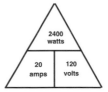

And since there is no such thing as a fraction of a spotlight — at least nothing you could use to light a show — that means our dimmer can safely control 4 spotlights (with 500-watt lamps)!

Bending Light

Before we look at the kinds of lighting instruments used in the theatre, let's take a quick peek at the two ways these instruments bend light rays. The two ways are called *reflection* and *refraction*.

We all know that mirrors reflect light — that's why we can see ourselves in them. Many of us have played with mirrors or other shiny surfaces and discovered that a beam of light directed at the mirror is reflected back at an angle equal to the angle at which it strikes the surface.

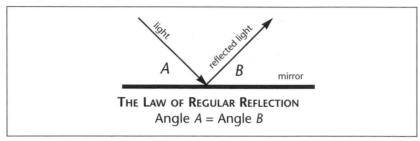

THE LAW OF REGULAR REFLECTION
Angle *A* = Angle *B*

This rule, called the *Law of Regular Reflection*, is what makes it possible to design reflectors for various stage lighting instruments. The reflector increases the efficiency of the instrument by sending more of the light produced by the lamp in the direction we want it to go. Without a reflector most of the light would be trapped inside the instrument, absorbed in the black paint frequently used there.

Modern lighting instruments usually use one of three reflector designs: *spherical, parabolic,* or *ellipsoidal.* Any one of them is better than no reflector at all. Which one is used in a particular kind of instrument depends on the size, shape, purpose, and cost of the instrument.

We know that curved mirrors do strange things to light. A *concave* mirror acts as a magnifier. A *convex* mirror, like those used on the sides of automobiles, reduces the size of objects reflected — but gives us a wider field of view. Those fun house mirrors distort what we see by magnifying some portions and reducing others. Reflectors for lighting instruments are all curved, but each curve is different, producing a different effect.

A spherical reflector is the simplest type. The reflector is really only a part of the sphere, like a small piece cut out of a ball. Since a sphere is a surface on which every point is equidistant from the center, a light source placed at the center, or focal point, of the sphere reflects light directly back through itself. Much of this light makes it all the way to the front of the instrument and then to the stage.

A parabolic reflector is a common sight to most of us. Radar and microwave antennae use this shape. So do the mirrors in the large telescopes used in astronomy. A parabolic reflector is curved so that light rays from a source placed at the focal point are reflected in a series of parallel lines — straight towards the front of the instrument.

The ellipsoidal reflector is based on the ellipse, a curve that's sort of like a circle with two centers. Light from a source at one focal point is reflected back through the other focal point. Since this reflector often surrounds the light source and captures more of the light from the lamp, it is the most efficient of the three.

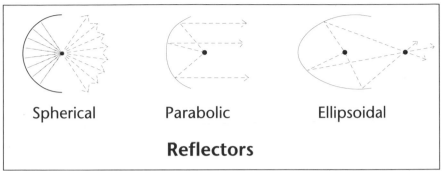

Spherical   **Parabolic**   **Ellipsoidal**

Reflectors

Most of us have noticed that a straw or spoon placed into a glass of water appears bent. This bending of light rays is called refraction, and it's what makes lenses possible and useful. Refraction, or bending of light occurs when light passes from a less-dense medium (like air) into a more-dense medium (like water, or glass). Refraction happens again when the light leaves the denser medium.

A *lens* is a piece of glass with one or two curved sides. The curvature determines the amount of refraction. A household magnifying glass has two curved sides. The lenses in lighting instruments have only one curved side. Since the curve is outward, it is called a convex curve. The other side is straight, or planar. A lens shaped like this is called *plano-convex.*

The lens of a lighting instrument is used to focus the light from the lamp and reflector, just as a magnifying glass can focus the rays of the sun. It allows the light to be aimed more accurately, with less spill or wasted light, so that a stronger beam of light reaches the stage.

The first spotlights developed for the stage used simple plano-convex lenses. The trouble with these designs was that a lens thick enough to focus the light was also so thick that it tended to break when the heat from the

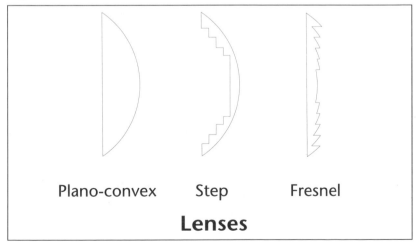

Plano-convex   **Step**   **Fresnel**

Lenses

lamp caused the nearer side of the lens to expand faster than the other side. The thickness of the glass also made it very heavy, increasing the weight of the instrument.

An early solution to these problems was the *step lens*. Much of the weight of the glass was removed by "hollowing out" the planar side of the lens, forming a series of steps. The heat-caused breakage problem was solved, too. But the lens still measured the same distance from front to back, limiting spotlight designers to longer instruments.

The third lens type reversed the idea of the step lens. The convex side of the lens was carved out into a series of smaller curves. This lens is widely used today because of its light weight and thinness. It's called a *Fresnel* (fruhnel´) lens, after the Frenchman who invented it.

Lighting Instruments

Stage lighting can be divided into two broad categories: *general lighting* and *specific lighting*. General lighting provides large expanses of the stage or the scenery (a drop or a sky cyclorama, for example) with a smooth and even wash of light. Specific lighting provides small areas of light which can be controlled independently of each other. Each category requires different kinds of lighting instruments.

General Lighting

General lighting uses two major types of lighting instruments: *strip lights* and *floodlights*. Let's take a quick look at both kinds.

Strip lights are long metal troughs, divided into sections. Each section contains one or two lamps, but no reflector or lens. The sections are electrically grouped so that every third (or every fourth) section is on the same circuit. That means that each circuit can use a different colored filter. If the three circuits use the three primary colors, red, green, and blue, a strip light connected to three dimmers can create a blend of almost any color. Strip lights are often used over the stage so that the color tone of the entire stage can be controlled. They are sometimes used to light drops. A variation of the strip light is found as footlights in older theatres.

Floodlights are large instruments consisting basically of a lamp socket surrounded by a reflector. Each floodlight contains one large lamp, frequently the same kind used in household lighting fixtures. There is no lens to focus the light, so the light spreads out quickly when it leaves the instrument. Because of its shape, the most common floodlight is called a scoop. There is a metal slot at the opening to hold a large sheet of color filter in a color frame.

Specific Lighting

Specific lighting uses spotlights to light the entire acting area or to light small parts of the stage, or even to light a single actor (even if he's married). There are two common types of spotlights: those that have a Fresnel lens and those that use an ellipsoidal reflector.

The spotlights with Fresnel lenses are called (you guessed it) Fresnels. A Fresnel is a metal box containing a lamp socket and parabolic reflector. The socket and reflector are mounted as a unit, so that they can be moved toward or away from the lens while maintaining the correct relationship to each other. Moving the lamp toward the lens causes the light beam to spread out wider, and moving it away from the lens creates a smaller beam of light. This adjustment is made from the bottom (on small Fresnels) or the back (on larger Fresnels) of the instrument. The Fresnel produces a soft-edged beam of light. Because its beam spreads fairly quickly, it is most often hung above the stage itself (as opposed to above the audience) to light upstage areas.

The other spot-light is not so easy to name. Sometimes they are called, simply, *ellipsoidals*. Other names include *Klieg light* (a trade name) and *Leko* (supposedly for a Mr. Levy and a Mr. Koch who developed them in the first place). These lights use one or two plano-convex lenses and produce a fairly narrow beam with hard edges. They have a set of built-in shutters that can be used to shape the beam. Some of these instruments are available with an iris (to

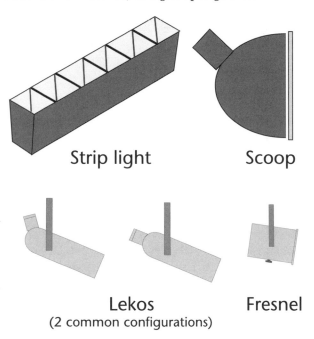

Strip light   **Scoop**

Lekos   **Fresnel**
(2 common configurations)

reduce the size of the beam while leaving it round) and/or a gobo slot (to insert small pieces of sheet metal, cut so they will project a pattern of light and shadow on the stage). Because it's easy to keep the light exactly where you want it (on the stage, but not on the proscenium arch or the front row of the audience, for example), these lights are commonly hung above the audience and used for lighting downstage areas.

Lamps

The first electric lights for the theatre used *incandescent* lamps. These lamps contain a tiny wire filament, made of a tungsten alloy, which heats up so much that it glows when electricity is passed through it. The filament is surrounded by a glass envelope from which all the air has been pumped. The air is removed to keep the filament from burning up as soon as the electricity is turned on, which it would do in the presence of oxygen. Advances have

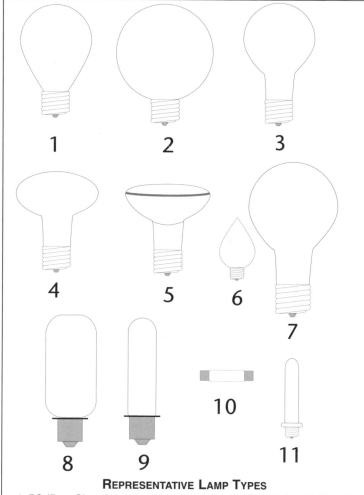

REPRESENTATIVE LAMP TYPES

1. PS (Pear Shape), medium screw base 2. G (Globe) 3. A (Arbitrary)
4. R (Reflector) 5. PAR (Parabolic Aluminized Reflector 6. C (Cone),
miniature screw base 7. A, mogul screw base 8. T-20 (Tube, 20 eighths
of an inch across), medium pre-focus base 9. T-12 10. Q (Quartz),
double-ended contacts 11. Q, miniature screw base

been made in lamp design, but the incandescent lamp is common in many (if not most) lighting instruments in use today.

The most modern lamp for theatrical use is the *quartz* lamp. This lamp, which does not use a tungsten filament, burns brighter longer, using less electricity. It also requires a smaller glass envelope, which allows designers and engineers to develop new, smaller, more efficient lighting instruments.

Lamps are classified according to the shape of the glass envelope and the type and size of their base. Some of the wide variety of lamp shapes are illustrated in the drawing below. The common light bulb has a medium screw base. Other types are the pre-focus base, and the bi-pin base. Some quartz lamps have one electrical contact at each end — sort of like an automotive fuse, or a flashlight battery. Sizes range from miniature to mogul.

The *T lamp* with a medium pre-focus base is widely used in Fresnels and Lekos. T lamps are further identified by a number (as in T–12 or T–20) that indicates the diameter of the glass envelope in eighths of an inch. A traditional Leko uses a T–12, which is twelve-eighths of an inch (1.5 inches) across, while a typical Fresnel uses a T–20 (2.5 inches across). Because of the design of the traditional instrument, the Leko lamp is designed to be burned with the base within 45º of up (BU +/- 45º). The T–20 is designed to meet the needs of the traditional Fresnel, and must be burned with the base down to horizontal (BDTH). Hanging either light so that the lamp base falls outside these limits results in the premature loss of the lamp, because the heat from the filament cannot escape as it needs to and actually softens the glass envelope.

These lamps contain filaments that must be lined up with the reflector and lens. The *pre-focus base* is designed so that the lamp can be inserted only one way (unless you're really determined). The two different-sized "ears" on the base must be matched to the two different-sized cutouts in the socket. The lamp is inserted, pushed down against a spring-loaded contact, and turned clockwise until it stops. It will stop turning in just the right place for the filament to be aligned with the reflector and **Pre-focus base** lens.

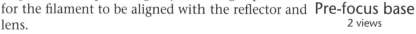

Pre-focus base
2 views

Heat is the inevitable by-product, and enemy, of lamps. A 500-watt lamp creates enough heat so that the entire instrument becomes "too hot to handle" after a short time. It is extremely important to keep lamps clean. Fingerprints left on a lamp will attract dust, creating a darkened area on the glass. This darkened area absorbs extra heat, causing a bubble in the glass. Eventually — but sooner than would have happened otherwise — the lamp burns out (and replacement lamps cost upwards of $50).

A Theory of Lighting Design

As we learned earlier in this chapter, the lighting designer's primary function is to provide visibility. Now we need to discuss a kind of specially defined visibility. Obviously, the actors would be visible if one gigantic spotlight were focused on the stage from straight ahead — at the actors' eye level. The trouble is they'd all look like deer caught in a car's headlights, or like prison photos.

Part of what we mean by visibility is making visible the shapes and contours of the people and things on the stage. Normal room lighting or outdoor sunlight reveals shapes and contours by causing shadows, and since the light is almost always from an overhead source we are accustomed to judging contours in this fashion.

What if we take our "one gigantic spotlight" and raise it so that it shines on the stage at a 45° angle? Will that create natural, contour-revealing shadows? Not exactly. It will create very dark shadows under the chins, noses and eyebrows of the actors, but it won't tell our eyes very much about the roundness of a cheek.

Suppose we move the spotlight so that it shines at a 45° angle to the side (as well as 45° up)? Aha! Surely this will solve the problem! Sorry, no such luck. The result this time is a little better — the roundness of noses and cheeks is revealed — but the shadows are so dark on one side of the face that it's like trying to see the back side of the moon.

All right. What if we use two spotlights, each 45° up and 45° out from the center of the stage? Well, now we've succeeded in erasing almost all of the shadows, hiding the shapes and contours again.

In the real world — as opposed to the stage — light from a single indoor light fixture bounces off the floor, the walls, the ceiling, and other objects. Outdoors, sunlight not only reflects off the ground and surrounding objects but it's dispersed by the air itself. (That's why sunlit photos of astronauts on the moon have such dark shadows: no atmosphere.) This reflected light acts to soften the shadows.

Stage settings seldom have ceilings, and much of the house and off-stage areas are purposely dark colored to absorb light rather than reflect it. And no spotlight yet developed is strong enough to duplicate the sun's trick of atmospheric diffusion! So what's a poor lighting designer to do?

Color comes to the rescue! If we leave our two spotlights in position but use a warm colored filter on one and a cool colored filter on the other, our brains will interpret the cool side of an actor's face as a shadow, even though it is brightly lit! The shapes and contours will be completely revealed, making the actors — and props and furniture and other set pieces — look three-dimensional rather than flat.

Area Cross-Lighting

To light the stage, divide it into separate areas, each one sized so that the beam from a single spotlight will cover it. Each area will be lighted using two spotlights. Each spotlight should be hung so that it's 45º above the stage and 45º to the side of the center of the area. A typical arrangement is shown in the drawing below.

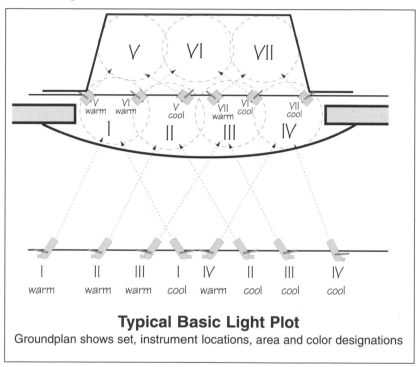

Typical Basic Light Plot

Groundplan shows set, instrument locations, area and color designations

Adaptations can be made to fit this plan to any setting on any stage. The number of areas might be changed to accommodate a deeper or shallower setting. The angles of the spotlights can be varied to fit the space available for hanging them, as well as the overall dimensions of the theatre.

Warm and Cool Colors

Most people think of red, yellow and orange as warm colors, and blue and purple as cool colors. Green is often thought of as neutral — depending on the specific shade of green under discussion. The important thing to remember as a lighting designer is that warm and cool are relative terms. Lavender is seen as warm when it's compared to a steel blue color, but it's definitely cool when compared to a pale straw (amber) color.

How does the designer decide which warm and cool colors to use?

Generally speaking, the colors are chosen so that they are complementary — when they are combined they create white light. The style and mood of the play determine whether to use a steel blue/pale straw combination, or a pinkish-amber/lavender combination, or one of the thousands of other possibilities. (Remember, the other designers for the show must be consulted, too!)

Our earlier discussions of color involved mostly the primaries and secondaries. The acting area is seldom lit with these colors, simply because they are so intense that the audience's eyes become tired quickly. Less intense colors have the same contour-revealing effect, and are easier on the eyes.

It's important that the shadows be consistent across the entire set. That means the warm colors should all come from the same side, as in the groundplan on page 91. Deciding which side to use for warm and which for cool is often influenced by the setting itself — it's part of the plausibility function of stage lighting. Consider a scene that takes place late at night in front of the glowing fireplace of a darkened mountain cabin. The warm lights should come from the same side as the wall of the set containing the fireplace, making it plausible that all (or most) of the light on the stage is coming from the fire itself. Windows, lamps, wall fixtures, chandeliers — the use and location of all these must be considered when assigning the direction from which the warm light will come.

> ## WHAT'S MY MOTIVATION?
>
> Speaking of windows, lamps, and fireplaces brings up the idea of *motivating* and *motivated* lights, a part of the lighting designer's arsenal of special effects. A window that is an apparent source of light requires two kinds of special lighting. The *motivating* light is the light (or lights) that shine directly on the backing outside the window, so the audience sees a blue sky, etc. The *motivated* light is a light that shines through the window from off-stage, causing a bright rectangle on the floor — just like sunshine! Other apparent light sources need a similar treatment.

Adapting to Other Stages

Two-color cross lighting can become three-color cross lighting in theatres where the audience surrounds the stage on three or four sides. Each area is lit by three spotlights, separated from each other by 120º. The three lights use a warm, a cool, and a neutral color so that the shadows will be cooler than the highlights no matter where you sit in the audience. This makes color selection even more important, and consistency even harder to maintain.

If the theatre has enough lighting instruments and dimmers, each area can use four spots. Matching the warm/cool aspects of the four lights is complicated, but it can be done.

Dimming the Lights

It wasn't long after theatres moved indoors and began using artificial light that attempts were made to control the intensity of the light on the stage. Through the candles and gaslights periods, dimmer control consisted of various mechanical devices to move some sort of light shield between the flame and the stage. When electricity moved in, true dimmers became possible.

The earliest dimmers worked by changing the amount of resistance in the circuit. (Remember that Ohm's Law and the PIE Formula show that changing the resistance while maintaining the same amperage will reduce the wattage of the lamp.) Resistance dimmers, whether they used metal resistors or even salt water, were bulky and heavy. It took muscle to move the dimmer control handle, and linking the handles together — to fade all the dimmers at once — created a real workout for the light crew. They also generated vast amounts of heat, forcing the use of cooling systems.

The *auto-transformer* dimmer operated on a different electrical principal. Since it reduced voltage to the lamp by using a variable transformer instead of a resistor, the heat problem was greatly reduced. Still, each dimmer needed to have its own handle or knob attached directly to it, and controlling several dimmers at once required the mechanical linking of the handles.

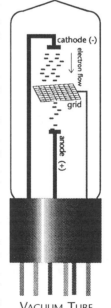

VACUUM TUBE

The first *electronic* dimmer used vacuum tubes. A small voltage applied to the grid of the tube controlled the amount of current flow through the tube. For the first time, the dimmer itself needed no handle or knob. It was possible to put the dimmers in the basement and keep the control panel in a position providing a view of the stage. The control panel and the dimmers could be connected by a cable made of small wires, since each wire needed to carry only a small amount of electricity, the control voltage.

The vacuum tubes used for dimmers — called thyratrons — were great producers of heat, and the heat often reduced their reliability. The newest generation of electronic dimmers seem to have solved all the problems. These dimmers use solid-state semiconductor technology (such as transistors, integrated circuits, etc.), which makes them much smaller and keeps heat from being a problem.

Called *silicon-controlled rectifiers*, they operate in a different way. Imagine that you could turn a light switch on and off so fast that you couldn't see the lights flicker. If the switch is off just as long and as often as it is on, the lights will be at half brightness. The rectifiers use a sort of electronic "gate" in place of the switch. This gate has the effect of turning the power on and off so fast that we can't see the flicker, and it allows the ratio between on time and off time to be varied from all off/no on, to no off/all on.

Electronic dimmers make it possible to have *proportional mastering*. This means that one dimmer set at 100% and another set at 50% can be dimmed together by a master control which will keep the first dimmer's lights twice as bright as the second dimmer's lights at any setting. Set the master at 80% and the two dimmers will be at 80% and 40%. Or set the master at 20% and the dimmers will be at 20% and 10% respectively.

Putting It Into Practice

Here's a quick guide to actually lighting a show. The steps in the guide should be followed carefully, adapting as needed to fit the requirements of the play and the equipment available in the theatre.

1. Read the script. Pay attention to the overall effect the play should have on the audience.

2. Read the script again, this time noting light cues ("Slow fade to black") and specific requirements for the lighting design ("The wind blows over the table lamp, casting the room into darkness.").

3. After conferring with the director, mark the light cues in the script. Indicate the exact cue for each lighting "event." Number each cue. Mark a WARNING for each cue half a page or so before the actual cue.

STUDIO THEATRE AT RINCON
LIGHT CUE SHEET

Show Title: _____   Page ____ of __

Cue #	Page #	DESCRIPTION	EXECUTE ON	DIRECTIONS

4. Fill out the CUE SHEETS for the show. Write down everything somebody else would need to know to run the show — just in case you're not available.

5. Obtain a copy of the groundplan for the set design. Draw the hanging positions available for lights, either on an overlay sheet (tracing paper through which you can see the groundplan) or directly on the groundplan.

6. On your overlay or groundplan, draw the lighting areas and instruments. Use roman numerals (I, II, III, IV, etc.) to identify the areas.

7. When all the instruments are on the drawing, use arabic numerals (1, 2, 3, 4, etc.) to number them consecutively. Begin with the lights farthest from the stage and work your way to the instrument in the last hanging position upstage. Don't forget any "practical fixtures," such as the lamp on the set that must be turned on and off in Act II. This is the *Instrument Number.*

STUDIO THEATRE AT RINCON								
INSTRUMENT SCHEDULE								
Show Title: _____					Page ____ of ____			
INSTRUMENT #	PLUG #	DIMMER #	PURPOSE	HANGING POSITION	INSTRUMENT TYPE	WATTS	COLOR	SPECIAL NOTES

8. Under each instrument, add the *Area Number* and color designation (W for warm, C for cool).

9. Transfer all this information to the INSTRUMENT SCHEDULE. I know, I know, you're infallible and you can remember it all, but it's vital to have everything written down so that the show doesn't depend on the continued good health and presence of one person.

10. Fill in the other columns of the INSTRUMENT SCHEDULE. If your theatre is hard-wired (each lighting position permanently wired to its assigned dimmer), the *Plug Number* and *Dimmer Number* will be the same. Otherwise, you can use the *Patch Panel* to assign each instrument to the dimmer you want. Be specific in the *Color* column: use the exact name/number designation of the filter color you'll use.

    Special Note: How many dimmers you have will determine what you can do with your lights. If you have enough dimmers to control each area separately (two instruments per dimmer), you will be able to vary the intensity of light by area. If you have fewer dimmers, you may have to group them differently — perhaps warms together and cools together to allow you to control the color tone of the stage. Ideally, you have one dimmer per spotlight, giving you both area and color control.

11. Hang the lights for the show according to the light plot and instrument schedule sheet. As each instrument is put into place and plugged in, aim it in the general direction it needs to shine and tighten it only "finger tight," to make the next step easier. This is also the time to set the patch panel, assigning each instrument to the correct dimmer.

12. Focus the lights. Use a wrench to tighten the bolts. Focusing lights is easiest with three people: the first to operate the dimmers (turning on only one light at a time makes it easier to see where it's shining and keeps the instruments from getting too hot to work with), the second on the ladder (or wherever the instrument can be reached), and the third on-stage. The third person stands in the center of the area being lit, directing the person on the ladder by looking for the "hot spot" in the center of the beam (sunglasses are nice, but not absolutely necessary!). Color filters should be added after focusing.

    Special Note: The circles you drew on the groundplan when you designed the lighting are only guides. The light won't make circles on the floor, it'll make ellipses. And besides that, you're not interested in lighting the floor (unless you're planning for a peculiar sort of tap-dancing exhibition, maybe). You need to focus the lights so that the actors are lighted, especially their faces. Think of what you're doing as lighting a volume of space instead of a circle on the floor.

13. Attend rehearsals. Get a feel for the show. Confer with the director about the speed of various fades — your actions in the light booth will have a

major effect on the audience's enjoyment and understanding of the play.

14. Set levels. This frequently occurs at the *First Technical Rehearsal*, but can happen any time. The director — and cast members or stand-ins — works with you to set the final dimmer settings for each scene of the play. Add these settings to your cue sheets.

15. Rehearse. Rehearse. Perform. Be sure you watch the stage whenever you execute a cue. Watching the dimmer control board won't tell you if the effect is actually taking place on the stage!

16. Your first job when you report to the theatre for tech rehearsals, dress rehearsals, and performances is to do an *Instrument Check*. Turn on all the lights and walk the stage, making sure that all the lights are working. Replace burned-out lamps or faded filters as needed.

Exercises:

1. Draw a poster showing the inner workings of a Fresnel and a Leko.

2. Read a one-act play and complete a lighting design as if it were to be produced on our stage. Include light plot, instrument schedule, and cue sheet(s). (Obtain script and forms from the teacher.)

3. Paint a poster that shows and identifies the effects of mixing colors, both pigment and light.

4. Illustrate the effects of colored light by painting a poster in such a way that the "picture" changes when the color of the light is changed.

CHAPTER ELEVEN

DOING THE DUO

This chapter tells how to prepare and perform a scene for two actors, a duo scene. It puts together some of the ideas from Chapters 2, 4, 6, and 8, so you may want to review that material before you get too far into this chapter.

Doing a duo scene requires you to use the skills and knowledge you have gained in earlier lessons. The improvisations you worked on (Chapter 4) gave you an idea of how to work with other actors, how to prepare yourself emotionally for a scene, and emphasized the importance of conflict and spontaneity. The monolog you prepared (Chapter 8) showed you the importance of understanding your script, preparing a groundplan, planning the blocking, and rehearsing (and rehearsing and rehearsing).

What's Different About a Duo?

Mostly, what's different is that you're working with somebody else, and the work usually extends over a longer period of time. Your ability to work together for a common goal is the key to success in a duo scene.

Choosing your partner is the first in a series of crucial decisions you must make. Your success (and your grade) will depend, at least in part, on the other person. No matter how hard your teacher tries to separate your performance from that of your partner when it comes time to be graded, the two of you will have influenced each other's performance throughout the rehearsal period. Such influences cannot be ignored by even the most experienced and most objective of teachers, because they form such an integral part of the fabric of the entire performance.

How do you pick a good partner? Most people jump right up and pick one of their friends to work with. It is important that you and your partner have or establish a friendly relationship, but in many cases a close friend is the worst possible choice. Sometimes it means that the two of you will have so much to talk about that you find it difficult to get down to work. You may even quarrel with a friend about things other than the scene, since we often seem to argue more often and more vigorously with those who are closest to us.

Does that mean you should just close your eyes and choose blindly? No, but it does mean that it's time for an honest examination of yourself and your work habits. If you know yourself to be serious about your work and motivated to do your best — and you believe your friend is the same — then by all means work together. If, on the other hand, you can recognize (and admit to yourself) that you have a tendency to procrastinate, to sit and talk about other things when you should be working — then don't choose your like-minded friend as a partner!

What a great rehearsal! You and Carol really got into that quarrel! Where did you find that "she stole my boyfriend" scene?

What rehearsal? She stole my boyfriend!

It goes without saying (but I'll say it anyway) that regular attendance is critical. Unless the two of you are able to get together on a regular basis outside of class, most of your work will be impossible when either of you is absent. Of course it's a double-edged sword: you choose a person whose attendance record and work habits will make him or her a dependable partner, and you make a commitment to your partner that you will attend every rehearsal — script and pencil in hand (or lines and blocking in head), ready to get to work!

The Rehearsal Process

Rehearsing a duo scene is a lot like rehearsing a monolog. Most of the steps are the same as those in Chapter 8. Additional steps, not appropriate when you're working alone, have been added to make your job easier.

1. Select a scene and choose a partner. Or choose a partner and select a scene — whichever is appropriate for the assignment in question.

2. Read through the scene with your partner. Make sure you both understand the words, and that you know what's going on in the scene. (You should read the entire play if a copy is available, but do it outside of class so that rehearsal time isn't wasted.) If the scene is for two characters of the same sex, you may want to read it twice, exchanging roles, before deciding who will play which part.

3. Determine the nature of the conflict. What does each character want in the scene? Be specific and concrete.

4. Draw a simple groundplan of your set.

5. Plan the blocking. Use your pencils to mark major movements and bits of business in your scripts.

6. Walk through the scene with scripts and pencils in your hands. Do the blocking as you planned, but be alert for problems, such as masking or upstaging each other, as well as opportunities to improve the scene.

7. Revise the blocking as necessary.

8. Go through the scene again to check the blocking.

9. Sit down face to face with your partner. Read through the scene slowly. Hold your script in your lap. Look at it long enough to put into short-term memory the first line (or the first sentence, or even the first part of the first sentence). Then look at your partner as you say those words. Return your eyes to the script to "get" the next group of words, then look at your partner again. Repeat this process until the scene is completed.

Never say a word until you are looking at each other!

Repeat this entire step, but this time look, think, and react before you say the words. Look at your partner to find something in his or her face that you can put into silent words ("She can't look me in the eye . . . what's she trying to hide?") before you say the words of the script.

This process is very slow, and it may be difficult for you to maintain concentration. But the payoff is worth it! It makes the scene alive, and also helps with memorization.

10. Return to the stage — or wherever you can set up your rehearsal — and go through the scene with the blocking. Make sure that *looking at the script* and *saying the lines* are kept as separate activities.

11. Go off book. As soon as possible, no later than half way through the rehearsal period, you must begin rehearsing without your scripts. At this point you should also begin working with props — either the

Self-Defense for the Actor

If somebody forgets a line during a performance, the audience probably won't know (or care) whose fault it is. All they'll know is that the scene has stalled and both actors look unprepared.

Protect yourself by being so familiar with the script that you know exactly what has to be done or said to get the scene moving again — from wherever it has stopped. The simplest way to accomplish this task is to learn *all* the lines in the scene, not just your own.

Fortunately, careful attention at rehearsal makes this easier than it sounds. In fact, it makes it almost automatic!

actual objects you'll use in performance or substitute props (a paper cup for a crystal goblet, for example).

Avoid the temptation to prompt each other in rehearsal because it's very difficult to stop doing it for your performance. (If your partner is absent for a rehearsal, maybe you could act as prompter for another duo.)

12. During a period when you don't think you can stand another run-through, take a break to write an introduction for your scene. It should involve both of you, and if it can be given as you are setting the stage it will save time and minimize boredom for the audience. The introduction needs to include your names, the title and author of the play, and any information about the setting or previous action that will help the audience understand what they're about to see. The introduction needs to be rehearsed until it's second nature, just like the rest of the scene.

13. Continue rehearsing. Remember that the purpose of rehearsal is two-fold: to build a "habit" of saying and doing the right words and actions, and to expand and deepen your understanding of your characters and their relationship with each other. This second purpose means that each rehearsal should be "better" than the one before; if you aren't making progress — if each run-through is an exact duplicate of the one before that and the one before that — you need to dig deeper into your characters' motivations, or find more concrete details in the setting or the previous action, or do something else to keep the scene from going stale.

14. At least the last five or six rehearsals should be done without a prompter or any other help with the lines. You need to practice "without a safety net" so that you'll be able to get yourselves out of any unexpected difficulties that crop up during your performance.

Performance and Evaluation

The last two steps of the process are exactly the same as they were for your monolog. Be prepared to perform. Execute your set-up and introduction efficiently and confidently. Avoid any kind of apology; make the audience feel safe and secure in the knowledge that you know what you're doing. Perform your scene, then gratefully acknowledge the applause and congratulations of your fellow students.

Exercises:

Prepare, rehearse, and perform a duo scene. Follow the directions given in this chapter.

CHAPTER TWELVE

FAMILY ALBUM, PART III
ELIZABETHAN AND FRENCH NEOCLASSIC THEATRE

The Renaissance in England and France

Not since the age of Aeschylus, Sophocles, and Euripides had the world seen such creativity in the theatre. When the Renaissance finally reached England, it created an explosion. It brought expanded knowledge of the Greek and Roman classics, but it also brought a new feeling of optimism, encouraging a scientific and geographical exploration of the world.

The invention of practical movable type by Johannes Gutenberg of Germany in the middle of the fifteenth century had made the world of knowledge available to everybody. Reading, once a skill known mainly by the clergy, became widespread. Along with it came an interest in history and national culture.

By the time Elizabeth I came to the throne in 1558, amateur and professional troupes of actors were performing widely. The liturgical dramas and cycle plays of the medieval period had been transformed into secular plays performed in schools, private banquet halls, and courtyards.

Public theatres catered to everybody: rich and poor, illiterate and learned, courtier and commoner. And make no mistake about it — acting companies and their playwrights were in it for the money. The successful companies worked hard to give the audience what it wanted. When interest in the history of England was most intense, historical chronicles took the stage. When interests changed, so did the plays being produced.

Elizabethan Playhouses

The public playhouses of Elizabethan London were lively places, teeming with activity. The shape and construction of the theatres influenced both the kinds of plays written and the way in which they were performed. The first theatre was called *The Theatre*. After it burned, *The Globe* and *The Swan* were built. The Globe was the home of *The Lord Chamberlain's Men,* the acting company whose playwright was William Shakespeare.

For many years we thought that all traces of the original wooden structures had long since disappeared. All we knew of them came from a couple of drawings (or copies of drawings) made by visitors to London, plus the words written about them by the playwrights. These drawings showed that the theatres were either round or polygonal (perhaps eight-sided) and were built around an open courtyard.

Recently, however, excavations in the old Bankside area of London unearthed the foundations of two theatres, including the Globe Theatre itself. The Globe was a structure with twenty-four sides or at least twenty gallery bays (no wonder the artists had trouble sketching the building!). The rebuilt Globe Theatre — except for underground and adjacent museums — will be just as it was during Shakespeare's day.

There were three galleries of seats surrounding the *yard* (later known as the *pit*), the open area where those who could afford only a penny stood during performances. These patrons were often called *groundlings*, because they stood on the ground. They were also called *penny stinkers*, because of their behavior. (All right, all right! Maybe it was also because they didn't bathe very often!)

At the Globe, the stage was about forty feet wide, extending about twenty-seven feet into the pit. The stage was probably raised at least five feet above the floor of the pit, improving visibility for the groundlings and making it possible to use the trap door in the stage for special effects, such as the appearance or disappearance of witches or spirits. The area under the stage was called *the hell,* and was possibly used as an early kind of echo chamber for the off-stage voices of invisible ghosts.

The stage had its own roof, at least sometimes called *the heavens*. A trap door in the ceiling allowed actors to be lowered to the stage from above. Between the two entrance doors at the rear of the stage was a small *inner stage* which could be closed off with a curtain. This area could be used for small scenes — in Juliet's chamber, for example, or Brutus' tent. A similar area was located just above, providing a setting for window or balcony or battlement scenes. Above that was a small thatch-roofed structure called the *hut*. The hoists for raising and lowering actors were located here, as were sound effects such as cannon and thunder sheets. Musicians for off-stage drum rolls and fanfares were stationed in the hut, too. Above the hut was a turret from which a flag was flown on performance days.

Performances

An open stage such as this, without much in the way of scenery and with lighting by sunlight, might seem limiting to those of us accustomed to modern plays — especially musical comedy — and films. The challenge was met head on, and turned into one of the Elizabethan theatre's greatest assets.

Because they didn't have to wait for complicated and lengthy movements of scenery, Elizabethan playwrights were free to move the action of their plays as often as they liked. Shakespeare's *Antony and Cleopatra* has more than forty scene changes! A few words from one of the characters at the beginning of a scene was all it took to establish the location of the scene. These speeches also took the place of stage lighting, indicating the time of day, the season, and the weather.

Historical accuracy in costuming was not important. Actors wore Elizabethan costumes for *Hamlet, Julius Cæsar,* and *Romeo and Juliet.* Each actor dressed as he saw fit.

There were no actresses in the Elizabethan theatre. Young men dressed up as women to play female roles. While this no doubt seemed quite natural at the time, it's probably at least part of the reason for the relatively small number of women's roles in the plays — as well as the shortage of scenes of physical intimacy between male and female characters. (It was also common for female characters to disguise themselves as men, creating a situation in which a man pretends to be a woman pretending to be a man!)

The openness of the stage — and the activity and noise that were very likely common in the pit — encouraged a more declamatory, less realistic style of acting than we are used to. Also, that might explain the many long and impassioned speeches in Elizabethan plays.

Playwrights and Plays

Ask anybody to name an Elizabethan playwright, and the odds are high that "Shakespeare" will be the answer. Most people, even drama students, are astonished to learn that even without Shakespeare, the Elizabethan stage would have been filled with exciting plots, wonderful characters, and beautiful poetic language.

The earliest of these brilliant playwrights were **John Lily** (1554?-1606), author of *Endymion, the Man in the Moon,* and **Thomas Kyd** (1558-1594), who wrote *The Spanish Tragedy,* a play of revenge.

The greatest of the early Elizabethans was **Christopher Marlowe** (1564-1593). Marlowe established *blank verse* as the standard for later plays in his earliest drama, *Tamburlaine the Great.* His best play is *Doctor Faustus,* a retelling of the German legend of the

BLANK VERSE?

Blank verse doesn't mean that the pages are empty. It's just the name given to poetry made up of non-rhyming lines containing five iambic feet. *(Forgive me for sounding like an English teacher, but an iambic foot is composed of two syllables: an unaccented one followed by an accented one — as in "To be or not to be. . . ." That's three iambic feet.)* Iambic pentameter is a very natural rhythm in English, allowing the verse to flow — even soar — in the hands of a master.

105

man who sells his soul to the devil in return for earthly knowledge and power. Here, as Faustus describes Helen of Troy's renowned beauty, we find a good example of "Marlowe's mighty line," as it was called by Ben Jonson:

Was this the face that launched a thousand ships,

And burned the topless towers of Illium?

Ben Jonson (1573?-1637), was also Shakespeare's contemporary. He was also one of the longest-lived of the Elizabethan playwrights — possibly because he avoided the taverns and their brawls that were the end of Christopher Marlowe. At one time, some people actually preferred Jonson's plays to Shakespeare's because they followed the forms of the ancient Greek and Roman plays. His plays include *Every Man in His Humour* and *The Alchemist*. His best known play is the comedy *Volpone*, in which a wealthy but selfish old man, with the help of Mosca, his servant, contrives to find out which of his relatives loves him the most — and will inherit his money — by pretending to be near death while putting the relatives through the wringer of his whims and wishes.

William Shakespeare, the Bard of Avon

It's true that the Elizabethan theatre had many excellent playwrights, but the world would have been immeasurably poorer had we been denied the presence of William Shakespeare. His plays have been performed, watched, and loved by millions of people all over the world, and they show every sign of continuing to be a source of genuine enjoyment for centuries to come.

Born at Stratford-on-Avon, probably on April 24, 1564 (he was baptised three days later), he was the son of a prosperous businessman and town official. He attended grammar school in Stratford and became apprenticed as a glover, his father's trade. At the age of eighteen he married twenty-six year old Anne Hathaway. A few years later, for reasons we'll probably never know, he left Stratford and his wife and three children and moved to London.

Shakespeare's activities during his first few years in London remain largely unknown. At some point he became one of *The Lord Chamberlain's Men,* a successful acting company. By the time he was twenty-eight years old he was recognized in print as both an actor and a playwright.

He continued to live and work in London for many years. When the plague kept the theatres closed for a time, he wrote the first of his sonnets and two long narrative poems. He lived and worked in an area northeast of London, where James Burbage managed two theatres, *The Rose* and *The Swan.* Between 1596 and 1597 he moved across the Thames River to the district known as Bankside, where Burbage built *The Globe* in 1598.

When Queen Elizabeth died in 1603, her successor, King James I, took

Shakespeare's company under his wing. They became known as *The King's Company*. In 1608 they acquired the *Blackfriars Theatre* — a smaller, more upscale theatre — and continued to perform plays at both locations.

Shakespeare retired from the theatre in 1610. The popularity of his plays — and his wise investments — made him a wealthy man. And a grant from the king made him legally a Gentleman. He returned to Stratford and lived at New Place, the largest home in the town.

Shakespeare died on April 23, 1616 at the age of 52. (Yes, he apparently died on the eve of his birthday, but remember that his birthday is only a guess based on the custom of taking an infant for baptism three days after the birth.) Shakespeare's body was buried in the chancel of the Church of the Holy Trinity in Stratford. (And as far as we know it's still there!)

Shakespeare's Plays

The plays of Shakespeare are generally divided into three categories: history, comedy, and tragedy. Since Shakespeare didn't know about this when he was writing, many of his plays seem to fit into more than one category, and some of them require sub-categories such as "dark (or bitter) comedy." In any event, these three make useful divisions for a brief look at his work.

Histories

Shakespeare met the intense interest of his countrymen in their history by writing several plays about English kings. He wrote *Richard II*, *Richard III*, *King John*, *Henry V*, and *Henry VIII*. Some of his subjects were so interesting that they required more than one play: *Henry IV, parts 1* and *2*; and *Henry VI, parts 1, 2*, and *3*. (Maybe Shakespeare was the inventor of that Hollywood staple, the sequel!) The great British actor Laurence Olivier made film versions of *Richard III* and *Henry V* in the 1940s. The fact that another film version of *Henry V* was made in the late 1980s suggests the enduring power of the play.

Richard III tells of the bloody rise to power of Richard Plantagenet, Duke of Gloucester. Richard liter-

Shakespeare *never* wrote a *classic* ...at least, not on purpose!

ally murders his way to the throne, killing everybody who stands in his way
— including his own brother, Clarence, and the two boy-princes. Somehow
Richard, portrayed as an ugly hunchback, persuades Anne, the widow of one
of his early victims, to marry him. King Richard is challenged by the forces
of the Duke of Richmond. During the battle Richard is unhorsed, and shouts
the famous line, "A horse! A horse! My kingdom for a horse!" Richmond
engages him in personal combat, kills him, and becomes King Henry VII.

Comedies

Shakespeare wrote at least sixteen comedies: *The Tempest, As You Like It,
The Winter's Tale, The Merchant of Venice, Twelfth Night, Much Ado About
Nothing, Cymbeline, A Midsummer Night's Dream, The Merry Wives of Windsor,
The Taming of the Shrew, Two Gentlemen of Verona, All's Well That Ends Well, A
Comedy of Errors, Pericles, Love's Labour's Lost,* and *Two Noble Kinsmen.* Then
there are the two dark or bitter comedies, *Measure for Measure* and *Troilus and
Cressida.* These plays cover a range of styles from farce to fantasy, from
coarse, bawdy humor to clever wit and word-play.

The Taming of the Shrew tells of Petruchio, a young gentleman down on
his luck, who agrees to marry Katherine, who is famous for her quick temper
and general shrewishness. He begins his courtship by insulting her, calling
her Kate, a nickname she despises. The more she attacks him — both ver-
bally and physically — the more he exclaims about her good manners and
gentle breeding. After the wedding, he takes her to his home where he
almost kills her with kindness: he rejects as unfit for her all food sent from
the kitchen as well as all clothing and all bedding. When he insists that it's
not day but night, she finally agrees, only to have him change his mind until
she agrees again. In the end the shrew is tamed, and Kate gives a final speech
almost guaranteed to offend a modern feminist with its insistence that a
wife's duty is to love, honor, obey — and even be a doormat for — her
husband.

Tragedies

Here's a list of Shakespeare's tragedies (notice that there are some
repeats from the list of histories): *Hamlet, Macbeth, King Lear, Othello, Antony
and Cleopatra, Coriolanus, Romeo and Juliet, Julius Cæsar, Richard II, Richard III,
Timon of Athens, King John, Titus Andronicus,* and *Henry VI.*

Shakespearean tragedy differs considerably from the Greek tragedies of
Æschylus, Sophocles, and Euripedes. Instead of adhering to the unities of
time, place, and action, Shakespeare allows his stories to roam freely, covering long spans of time and often including subplots. His heroes do have
tragic flaws, but sometimes (as in *Richard III*) it's difficult to see them as the
"basically good men" of Greek tragedy.

King Lear shows us a foolish old king who decides to divide his kingdom among his three daughters before his death. When he asks each of them to tell how much they love him, two daughters, Regan and Goneril, fill his ears with extravagant protestations of love, while the third insists she loves him no more than is her duty. Finding her behavior "sharper than a serpent's tooth...," he gives Cordelia nothing. It's not too long before the old man is tossed out on his ear by his two "loving" daughters. He realizes just before his death that Cordelia loved him best of all.

On Reading Shakespeare

If the thought of reading Shakespeare sends shivers down your spine — and they're not shivers of delightful anticipation — keep this in mind: Shakespeare was the Steven Spielberg or Francis Ford Coppola of his day. He wrote plays to be enjoyed by all kinds of people, and none of them considered him a *classic*, to be approached with awe and reverence. It's true that our language has changed since Shakespeare wrote, but the basic facts of human nature — and the masterful way Shakespeare exposes them to our view—haven't changed a bit.

Most American high school students read one or more of the following plays: *Macbeth, As You Like It, Julius Cæsar, Hamlet, Romeo and Juliet, The Merchant of Venice, A Midsummer Night's Dream, The Tempest,* and *Twelfth Night.* Any of these make a good place to start for a new reader of Shakespeare.

Shakespeare's use of verse should not put you off. Most of it flows smoothly and beautifully — and it's an actor's dream. Read aloud this speech of Prospero from *The Tempest*:

> Our revels now are ended. These our actors,
> As I foretold you, were all spirits, and
> Like the baseless fabric of this vision,
> The cloud-capp'd towers, the gorgeous palaces,
> The solemn temples, the great globe itself,
> Yea, all which it inherit, shall dissolve
> And, like this insubstantial pageant faded,
> Leave not a rack behind. We are such stuff
> As dreams are made on, and our little life
> Is rounded with a sleep.

Theatre of the French Renaissance

The renaissance came with a bang to France, too. Its impact on the French theatre was startling. French theatre of this period lacked the wide popular appeal of the Elizabethan theatre. The best playwrights and actors worked in smaller, indoor theatres where performances were given for the elite of the court and society. A wave of *neoclassicism*, imitation of the newly rediscovered works of the Greeks and Romans, was exemplified in the works of two playwrights: **Pierre Corneille** and **Jean Racine**.

Corneille (1606-1684) began his career with a comedy of manners called *Melité* in 1629, but quickly adopted a more classical orientation. His tragedies *Medea, Horace,* and *The Death of Pompey* rigidly adhere to the unities of time, space, and action. His most popular play, *Le Cid,* based on the adventures of the legendary Spanish hero, was more romantic in style, breaking the supposed rules of classicism.

Racine (1639-1699) challenged Corneille's place as the leader of French theatre. His tragedies *Britannicus, Iphigenia in Aulis,* and *Phedre* won the younger playwright a place of honor. Many believe that Racine humanized French tragedy in much the same way that Sophocles and Euripedes did the Greek. It has been said that Corneille showed men as they ought to be, while Racine showed them as they are.

Molière was the pen name of Jean Baptiste Poquelin (1622-1673). He was the author of many comedies. His satires of current figures and popular culture were often criticized and sometimes banned from the stage. He was an actor and director as well as a playwright, and, like Shakespeare, was a master of showmanship. His most famous plays include *The School for Wives, Tartuffe, Don Juan, The Miser, The Doctor in Spite of Himself,* and *The Imaginary Invalid.*

The Imaginary Invalid is the story of a confirmed hypochondriac, Argan. His wily servant helps Argan's daughter dupe her father into giving permission for her to marry. Much fun is poked at the invalid, as well as at unscrupulous quacks posing as reputable doctors. Molière supposedly collapsed while performing the role of the hypochondriac and died later the same day.

Exercises:

1. Construct a model or paint a poster of an Elizabethan playhouse.

2. Write a biography of Christopher Marlowe, Ben Jonson, James Burbage, or Molière.

3. Read *Volpone, Dr. Faustus*, a Molière comedy or any Shakespeare play *not assigned for your English class* and report on it to the class.

4. Memorize a speech (approximately twenty-five lines) from any of Shakespeare's plays. Recite it to the class.

5. Make a poster showing the English kings and their family relationships (sort of like a family tree) from Richard the Lionheart to Elizabeth I.

CHAPTER THIRTEEN
THEATRICAL MAKEUP

Since the first actor stepped into the circle of light around the campfire to re-enact the successful hunt, since the first performance at the Theatre Dionysus in Athens, since Shakespeare trod the boards at The Globe — well, you get the idea — actors have understood the importance of the way they look. They know that the audience will judge them not only by their actions but by their appearance.

No matter how talented and hard working the actor may be, no matter how wonderfully the voice and gestures and movements fit the forty-year-old highly paid executive from Seattle who suffers from nearsightedness — if the face and hands (and *all* the visible skin areas) look more like a teenager from the sunbelt, the audience will have to fight for that "willing suspension of disbelief" that is the *sine qua non,* the absolute necessity, of effective characterization. And we certainly don't want the audience to have to struggle to enjoy our performances, do we?

Preparing effective makeup is an important process, and one that should be mastered by every actor, especially those who want to work in the legitimate theatre. Makeup artists are routinely provided in the television and movie industries, but almost never provided for stage actors. And, as the old saying goes, if you want something done right, do it yourself!

Making yourself look like somebody else — a character in a play — is a two-part process: deciding how the character should look, and applying the makeup to accomplish that effect. Let's take a look at each of these topics.

Character Analysis

"All you _____ are just alike!" (Fill in the blank with any one of the following: children, teenagers, men, women, students, teachers, parents, retired people, southerners, westerners, Yankees, Americans, immigrants, Mexicans, Chicanos, Asians, Europeans, Anglos...and so on and on and on.) The point is, of course, that nobody likes to be lumped together with an entire category of people simply because of one or two common characteristics. Students are *not* all alike. Teachers are *not* all alike. Parents are *not* all alike. Retirees are *not* all alike. And so on and on and on!

In order to create a unique characterization — in makeup as well as in acting — you need to analyze the character, to figure out what makes this character different from all other characters. In other words, be specific!

What are the factors that make every person/character different from every other?

H.E.A.R.T.H.

The word **hearth** is a *mnemonic* device to help you remember the six elements of character analysis. Each letter stands for one of the six elements: heredity, environment, age, race, temperament, and health. Each of these elements affects the appearance of a person — in life or in a play.

Heredity refers to those characteristics that are inherited from our parents and grandparents — our family traits. Heredity is important if you are playing a character who is the blood relative of another character in the play. In *Life With Father*, by Lindsay and Crouse, it's important that the children all have the same red hair as their father. Sometimes, of course, children don't look much like their parents, and brothers or sisters have little resemblance to each other.

> ### STRAIGHT MAKEUP VS. CHARACTER MAKEUP
>
> Those who have never studied theatrical makeup sometimes think there are only two kinds: *straight* makeup — when the character is of the same age range and general appearance as the actor — and *character* makeup — when the character and the actor obviously differ in age and/or other characteristics. Wrong!
>
> Unless your friend the playwright has written a part *especially for you* — just like you in every detail — you need to analyze the character, discovering the specific ways in which the character's appearance differs from your own.
>
> Once in a while (for a talent show or an interview on television, for example) a performer needs *corrective* makeup so that his or her own appearance will be as good as possible under the bright lights that tend to make faces look washed out and flat. That's as close as we get to straight makeup!

Environment plays a large part in determining a person's appearance. A librarian and a lumberjack look different, at least partly because one works indoors, the other outdoors. A wealthy woman who spends her life shopping and traveling will look very different from a woman who works every day in a fast-food restaurant and every night in an office building cleaning floors. A Floridian will differ from a Minnesotan — even if their jobs are similar — simply because of the vast difference in the amount of sunshine in the two states. Environment also includes a time element: a deep tan is much less fashionable today than it was only a few years ago, a "peaches and cream" complexion was highly desirable a hundred years ago, and the favored skin tone of the Restoration period was what we'd call a pasty white!

Age can be deceptive. A person's chronological age is only one part of the appearance equation. Not all fifty-year-olds look alike. The apparent age is influenced by heredity (prematurely gray hair, male pattern baldness), environment (sun– or wind–caused wrinkles), health (chronic illness ages a person quickly), temperament (frown–caused wrinkles), to give just a few examples.

Race is an important factor, too. Nowadays it is less common than it used to be for actors to play members of other races. Still, there are some plays and some places where it's important to understand the appearance-related characteristics of major racial groups.

> **"IN GENERAL" IS THE ENEMY OF GOOD MAKEUP, GOOD THEATRE, AND ALL GOOD ART.**

Temperament is the term we'll use for *personality.* A face reveals the emotional character of its owner. A person who smiles frequently tends to acquire those little wrinkles at the corners of the eyes we often call "crow's feet." A person who frowns all the time develops a frown line — the vertical wrinkle between the eyebrows. A person who expresses very little emotion — and who stays out of the sun and wind — usually has very few wrinkles.

Health affects a person's looks in many ways. There are two categories of ill health that need separate consideration: acute illness and chronic illness. Sometimes a character in a play suffers from an acute illness such as a cold or the measles or seasickness. Sometimes a character pretends an acute illness. It's important that you know the visible symptoms of whatever disease is involved. A character sometimes suffers from a chronic illness, one of long duration or frequent recurrence, such as arthritis, asthma, multiple sclerosis, or diabetes. These diseases, too, can create specific visible signs (such as a jaundiced — yellowish — complexion) that are a part of a character's "look."

The actor's makeup analysis must include each of the **hearth** elements. Some elements are less important than others for some characters and some plays and some productions, but all elements must be at least *considered* for every character. Where does an actor find information for this analysis?

Character Research

We'll make this short and sweet, because the same information has been mentioned in Chapter 7. There are three basic sources of information about a character: what the playwright says about the character (and the place and time of the play) in stage directions or descriptions, what the character says about himself or herself, and what the other characters in the play say about the character in question. So far so good! But there's an important addendum to each of those three.

First, many plays identify their time period only as "The Present." If you're acting in an actual production, the director and designers will have decided upon a specific setting (and sometimes it's far removed from the "expected" setting... Shakespeare's *The Tempest* has been done as science fiction, with a spaceship replacing the sailing vessel of the original script), but if you are preparing a character analysis and makeup for practice the decision is yours. One good clue is to find the copyright or first publication date of the play — this will identify what the playwright meant by "The Present." This particular source won't be of much help for plays old enough to have been reprinted many times — such as *Our American Cousin* or *All's Well That Ends Well* — or those translated from other languages — such as *The Cherry Orchard* or *Rosmersholm*. The solution in these cases is to discover the time in which the play was written by (shudder) looking up the play or the playwright in another book! That

MCMXLVI?

Finding the copyright date may be only half the battle if you can't read roman numerals. (Roman numerals are an invention of publishers and filmmakers, designed to keep their readers and viewers in the dark about exactly how old a book or movie really is.) Here's a brief explanation.

Each letter stands for the particular number shown below.

$$I = 1$$
$$V = 5$$
$$X = 10$$
$$L = 50$$
$$C = 100$$
$$D = 500$$
$$M = 1,000$$

A smaller number placed after a larger number is added to the larger amount. The smaller number is subtracted from a larger following number (IV equals 4, LX equals 60).

That means that MCMXLVI is broken down to M = 1000, CM = 900, XL = 40, and VI = 6. Line them up and you have 1946. (Why couldn't they just say so in the first place?)

should do it, unless you're dealing with a play written in one time period but set in another, like Shakespeare's *Julius Cæsar* (which was originally performed wearing costumes of Shakespeare's day, not the Roman Empire). In those cases, you'll have to be very creative — or ask for help from your instructor!

Remember to read carefully before you accept as true any statements made by characters in plays. Sometimes characters lie. Sometimes they exaggerate. Just because a character speaks of himself as "tall, dark, and handsome" doesn't mean it's true — any more than another character's description of him as "a washed-out little pipsqueak." You must take *everything* into account, including the motives of the characters!

Facial Anatomy

A clear understanding of the structure of the human face is vital to planning and executing good theatrical makeup. Knowledge of the underlying bone structure, its prominences and depressions, gives the actor/makeup artist a clear picture of what's possible in working with a specific face and what's most likely when studying a specific character.

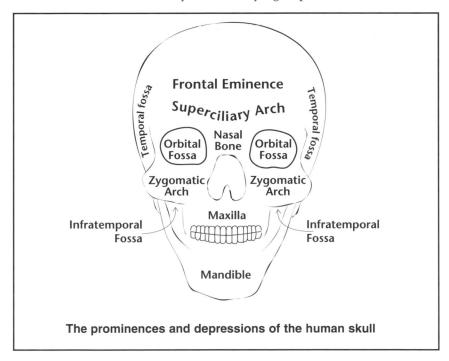

The prominences and depressions of the human skull

Study the diagram above. Use your eyes and your fingers to locate each of the prominences and depressions on your own face. Learn the names, because many of the following discussions will use these terms, taking it for granted that you know them!

The Changing Face of...

Ever wonder what you'll look like when you're fifty or sixty or seventy? A basic understanding of the aging process — and a few sessions in the makeup lab — will give you a pretty good idea!

A youthful face, with its smooth skin and firm jaw, has four major enemies: time, gravity, sunlight, and emotion. Over the course of years, these four elements combine to give a face what's sometimes called *character*.

With the passing years, our muscles and connective tissues lose their resilience. The muscles in our faces that we use the most often retain strength and flexibility longer than those used less often. These under-used muscles tend to stretch and sag due to the relentless effect of gravity pulling down on them. And why are some muscles used more than others? That's where sunshine and emotion come into play. Our faces reflect our emotional states. If we laugh, we use one set of muscles. Frowning uses a different set. Squinting — often caused by sun and wind — uses a particular group of muscles. Just as in weight training or body building, frequent exercise with small weight but many repetitions causes muscles to be strong *and* well-defined. The combination of these factors, together with inherited traits, creates the particular pattern of wrinkles and folds that identify an older face.

Getting Specific

Let's take a look at specific parts of the face and how they are affected by the aging process.

The frontal eminence often becomes more pronounced with age, as does the superciliary arch. The temporal fossæ usually become more obvious, too. Crow's feet, the wrinkles that fan out from the outside corners of the eyes, are a very common effect of aging. The zygomatic arch becomes more prominent, and the naso-labial folds (from the corners of the nose to the outside of the mouth) become deeper. As the skin sags, the planes of the nose become even more visible. Other individual features such as a cleft chin, present in youth, become more prominent. Sunken eyes will appear to retreat even farther into the orbital fossæ.

Lips get thinner and lose their natural color. The jaw line is blurred, especially in those with fuller faces, by sagging muscles creating what we call jowls. Eyelids sometimes sag and droop, too.

The complexion changes, too, depending upon the specific person. In men, beards often get thicker and heavier before they go grey. Women and men alike acquire various scars and discolorations as they age. Heavy drinkers often have a reddened nose or cheeks caused by the breakage of tiny blood vessels, called capillaries, near the surface of the skin.

Physiognomy

Physiognomy (pronounced *fizz-ee-ahg´-nuh-mee*) is the practice of judging a person's character by looking at his or her facial features. I know,

I know: you can't judge a book by its cover. But it's something we all do all the time. We associate certain character traits and emotions with certain features, and we judge the person accordingly — sometimes to our great and everlasting loss!

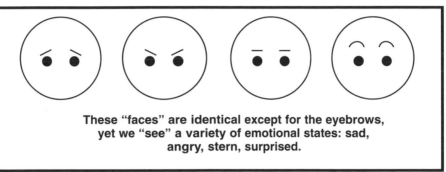

**These "faces" are identical except for the eyebrows,
yet we "see" a variety of emotional states: sad,
angry, stern, surprised.**

Facial features have great power in conveying information (or misinformation) about a person. This power is shown in cartoons, where a few strokes of the cartoonist's pen are often enough to provide the viewer with an immediate and strong indication of the drawing's emotion and character.

We won't take the time and space needed for anything like a complete discussion of physiognomy — it would take many pages. We can mention just enough to spark your interest. Please keep in mind that the "messages" of individual features are greatly influenced by other features. The face must be considered as whole.

The Forehead

A high forehead or receding hairline is often associated with high intelligence. This applies to both men and women, but probably is stronger in men.

Frown lines are attributed to one of two general causes. A frown line might signify a bad-tempered person, but it might also indicate a person who spends a great deal of time in deep concentration.

The Eyes

"The eyes are the windows on the soul." ...So goes the old saying, and the eyes — or the muscles in the area around the eyes — certainly do convey a great deal of information about a person.

Prominent eyes are generally considered an attribute of an æsthete or dreamer, while deep-set eyes are associated with an analytical turn of mind. Close set eyes, especially if they are small, are often taken to be an indication of dishonesty. Large, well-spaced eyes are a sign of a trustworthy person.

Crow's feet may indicate a happy person who smiles or laughs frequently — or they might just mean that this person spends a great deal of time outdoors in the sun and wind.

Full eyebrows are often taken to be a sign of a forceful person, while thinner eyebrows may indicate a weak or passive personality. Bushy eyebrows with hairs going in all directions signal a disorganized mind. Eyebrows close to the eyes — particularly if they meet or almost meet in the middle — are thought to be a sign of low cunning and a mean spirit. High, arched brows may mean a gullible person of little intelligence.

The Nose

Noses come in many shapes and sizes. They are straight or curved, knobby or smooth, long or short, turned down or turned up, wide or narrow or broken. Generally speaking, larger noses are indications of strength and leadership. Long, narrow aquiline noses often suggest a person of refined taste. A bulbous nose, one with a large, rounded tip, denotes dissipation, especially if it is reddened.

Because the nose and ears are the last parts of the body to stop growing (usually sometime in a person's fourth decade of life), a longer nose often denotes age. A pointy nose signals a nosy person. A bent nose is associated with rough, physical types — apt to have engaged in fist fights.

The Mouth and Lips

A wide mouth points to a generous person, while a small mouth argues that the owner may be as tight-fisted as he or she is close-mouthed. Full lips hint at a sensuous nature; thin lips imply a strict temperament.

The Chin

A strong chin suggests a strong and aggressive personality. The owner of a weak or receding chin is most often seen as weak-willed and passive.

Cheeks

Round red cheeks belong to jolly people. Thin or sunken cheeks may signal a businesslike person who has little time for life's pleasures. A pronounced wrinkle about halfway between the mouth and ear (called the jugal fold) indicates a streak of cruelty.

Seeing the Shapes of the Face

A glance at a face is all we need. Almost immediately we know that this face has a narrow nose, deep-set eyes, and sunken cheeks, or that face has a wide nose and full cheeks, or the other face has full lips, deep naso-labial folds, and prominent eyes. In other words, we see more than the color and general outline of the face, we see its depth.

Human beings have binocular vision — two eyes that focus together, enabling us to see in three dimensions, to have depth perception. When you're gazing into the eyes of your "significant other" — or looking at any other face up close — your depth perception is at work, but our eyes are not all that far apart, which means that the three-dimensional effect weakens rapidly as the face moves further away. A face as close as eight or ten feet is too far away for our eyes to produce true depth perception.

So...exactly how do we "see" the depth of a face? Highlights and shadows! We are accustomed to the normal patterns of light and shadow on faces, and when a face is too far away for binocular vision to provide clues, we rely on the positions and sizes of the highlights and shadows to reveal the three-dimensional structure of the face. This is great news for the theatrical makeup artist, because it means that by simply painting shadows and highlights where we want them, we can fool the eyes of the audience into seeing shapes that are not really there!

Mind Your Eyes!

It's important that you begin to pay attention (with your mind) to the faces you see (with your eyes). Start with your own face! Look into a mirror and notice the highlight that runs down the middle of your nose, and the slight shadows on the sides of your nose. See the highlights on your zygomatic arches. If you're too young for wrinkles, you can almost always force temporary ones to appear by stretching and scrinching up your face. Grin widely and look for the shadows and highlights that define your own naso-labial folds. Squint and frown to see crows feet

FOOLING OUR EYES

Makeup artists aren't the only ones in theatre who depend on false highlights and shadows. Scene designers and painters use this technique, too. A perfectly flat object can appear to have depth by painting just

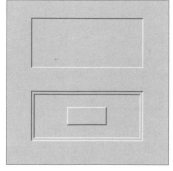

a few lines, like this. Because we are accustomed to seeing objects lighted from above, we'll see a depression or hole or recess if we use the "shadow color" to draw lines at top and one side, and the "highlight color" on the bottom and opposite side. Reverse the colors to create a raised area.

and frown lines. Where do the shadows appear in relation to the highlights (assuming that the light on your face comes from above)?

Study pictures of other people. Many actors keep a collection of people-pictures called a **makeup morgue**. The pictures are usually cut out of magazines, etc., and carefully attached to stiff paper with rubber cement. Small morgues, or sections of larger ones, are frequently kept in three-ring binders, organized into categories such as *children, teens, adults, old age, racial types,* and so on. A well-maintained morgue is an extremely useful resource for the actor/makeup artist.

Practicing With Highlights and Shadows

Before you start putting makeup on your face, learn how to use highlights and shadows to fool the eye. You can begin your practice with nothing more complicated than a sheet of white paper and a soft lead pencil with an eraser.

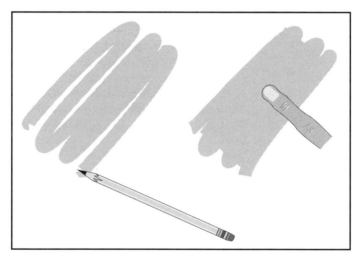

It's easier to work with a background that's not the pure white of the paper, because you can use the eraser to create highlights. First, use the side of the pencil lead to draw a series of wide, soft, overlapping, light gray lines. Next, use your finger to rub the area until the light gray is evenly spread. (The graphite will also cover your fingertip, so be sure to wash your hands before going ahead to the next step.)

Use the point or the edge of the pencil lead to draw a shadow that begins very dark and gradually fades to almost the same shade as your background. (Placing another sheet of paper between your drawing hand and your drawing will help protect your work from smudging.) Use the eraser to create a highlight that is strongest where it meets the darkest area of the shadow and fades gradually until it is barely lighter than the background.

Remember the old saying: "If at first you don't succeed, try, try again!" If success eludes you at first, *don't give up!* Move to another area of your background and try again! Experiment with curved or rounded shapes, too. Try drawing something like the picture at right. It shows the correct relationship between highlight and shadow for a crease or wrinkle on a face. (Yes! The highlights are below the shadows when the light source is above the face — as it almost always is.)

Have fun! Experiment! Play around with your pencil, eraser, and paper. Soon you'll be ready to move to drawings of the face. Your teacher may provide you with copies of the blank face, or you can make your own photocopies. If you want to save the money, you can trace the face shown on page 124.

The process is basically the same, as shown in the sequence below, but this time you're working to give a three-dimensional effect to a face. Again, don't be afraid to experiment with your tools.

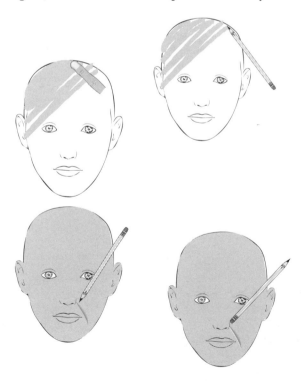

Here's a blank face for you to copy. Use your copy to practice shading and highlighting. You will prepare a finished drawing of the specific character you're playing in the final stages of your analysis and planning process.

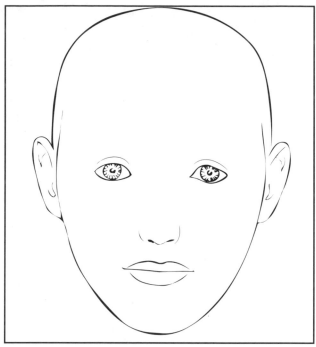

Blank face for planning a makeup job. Below is a sample of a completed drawing.

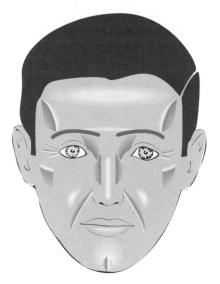

In the Makeup Lab

Finally it's time to work with more than pencil and paper. You're about to put your makeup where your mouth is. Also where your nose and eyes are! One last item remains, and it's important to understand before you jump in with sponges and brushes flying.

Modern actors use one of three different kinds of makeup: grease paint, pancake, or creme. Each kind has its advantages and disadvantages.

Grease paint is the oldest of the modern makeups. It consists of various pigments (colors) mixed into an oil base. It is usually purchased in tubes (like the oil paints used by artists) or small tins. The advantages of grease paint are that colors can be mixed and blended easily, and it totally covers the actor's skin, allowing radical changes in skin tone or even skin color. The disadvantages are that it seals the pores and sweat glands, frequently causing the actor to sweat and itch (and you can't scratch because you'll ruin the makeup, even after it's been "set" with powder), and cold cream or a similar product is needed to remove it. It's also true that most people dislike applying anything oily to sensitive skin.

Pancake makeup is dry. It's sold in flat, compact-like plastic containers. It's applied with water (dampened sponges and brushes). It's easy to remove (soap and water), it requires no powder to "set" it, and it doesn't clog the pores of the skin. Once applied, however, mistakes are difficult to cover up — usually you have to wash off the mistake and start over — and blending or shading colors on the face is difficult.

Creme-type makeups are the latest to become popular. They share some of the qualities of both grease paint and pancake. Although powder is required to set the makeup and colors are easy to blend, it is a water-based (non-oily) product that is applied with fingers, sponges, or brushes without additional water. And it washes off with soap and water!

Applying Your Makeup

This section should be used as a guide for a series of makeup labs. As you work your way through the list, allow yourself plenty of time for trial and error, and remember the old saying: "If at first you don't succeed, try, try again!" Remember, too, that you'll need time to clean up (both your face *and* your space in the lab) at the end of each session in the lab.

Read (and understand) each section all the way through before you begin applying the makeup.

Base or Foundation: Creme-type makeup is applied with your fingers or a small sponge. Take up a small amount of makeup on your applicator of choice and apply small dabs all over your face. Once the dabs of makeup are applied, use your fingertips to blend them into a smooth covering over the entire face. Too much makeup will result in an unpleasant caked-on look. (Remember that makeup should be applied to all areas of visible skin, such as your neck and ears, but for purposes of practice in a lab of limited time, it is permissible to restrict the application to your face only.)

Naso-labial folds: These are the large creases that begin at the corners of the nose and continue downward and outward beyond the corners of the mouth. They are the largest "wrinkles" on most people's faces — especially young people — making them the easiest place to learn the basic technique of painting wrinkles. Take up a small amount of shadow color with the brush. Holding the brush perpendicular to your face, use the *end* to draw a narrow, dark line at the deepest part of the crease. Then use the side of the brush to soften or draw out the outside edge of the line. Be

Drawing a line with the end of the brush

sure that the line has a soft edge on the outside and a hard, sharp edge on the inside. The total width of the line determines the apparent depth of the fold. The line must come to a point at both ends. Next, apply a narrow highlight along the inside (hard) edge of the shadow. Don't let the highlight color

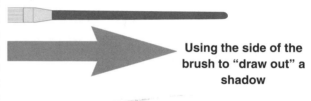

Using the side of the brush to "draw out" a shadow

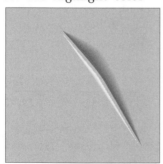

mix with the shadow color. The highlight must have a hard edge next to the hard edge of the shadow. Soften the other edge of the highlight (toward the center of the face). Last, apply a soft highlight to the front part of the cheek, using your fingers to blend the edges so that they fade into the base coat all the way around.

Crow's feet: These are the small wrinkles that radiate outward from the corners of the eyes. They are sometimes called laugh lines. They are applied in the same way as naso-labial folds, just smaller: each wrinkle has a shadow above and a highlight below, with hard edges that meet and soft edges that blend away from the center of the wrinkle. Be sure to paint these wrinkles — and all others — only in places where they naturally occur. You may need to squint, or even use a finger and thumb to pinch the corners of your eyes together to find where they fall on your face.

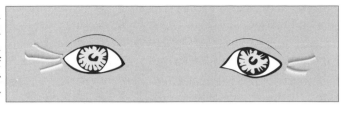

Nose: The size and shape of the nose reveals many personality traits to the audience. They perceive the size and shape of the nose by looking at the shadows and highlights. Basic shading principles apply: dark colors recede,

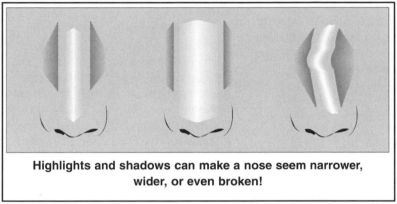

Highlights and shadows can make a nose seem narrower, wider, or even broken!

light colors advance. To make your nose appear narrower than it is, apply shadow color to the sides of your nose beginning above the edge of the ridge of cartilage that forms the length of the nose; then apply a narrow highlight down the center of the nose. To make your nose appear broader, apply the shadow color well down on the sides of the nose and apply the highlight so that it extends to the sides of the central ridge of the nose — where the shadow naturally falls. A broken nose can be simulated by painting crooked shadow and highlight lines.

Eyes: To make the eyes appear deep set, apply shadow color to the inside upper corners, next to the nose. Prominent eyes are achieved by using a highlight color instead of a shadow color in the same places. Notice that shadows here also tend to make the eyes appear closer together, while highlights seem to move the eyes farther apart. Bags under the eyes can best be achieved by imitating a photograph of the real thing. Essentially, a bag or pouch under the eye consists of a fairly deep

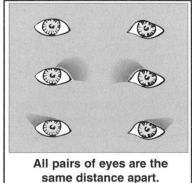

All pairs of eyes are the same distance apart.

127

wrinkle — hard edge away from the eye — with a sharp highlight below it and a subtle highlight above.

Eye Liner: The application of a shadow color (or another color) at the base of the eye lashes serves to accentuate the eyes, and is very frequently necessary — even for male characters — when the theatre is large or the character is young or the play is in any way nonrealistic. As in making wrinkles, use the end of the brush to paint a thin line. Unless you are playing an ancient Egyptian or maybe a silent movie star, never outline the whole eye. A good rule of thumb is to line the entire upper lid and only the outer half of the lower lid. Experiment with different line lengths, and with allowing the lines to meet at the outside corner of the eye or leaving a tiny open space. Application of

DETAILS OF DISGUISE

If you are playing an older character, be aware that wrinkles alone are not enough! Two things signal an audience most strongly that they are looking at a young face with painted wrinkles: smooth unblemished skin, and a firm jaw line. Go back to your morgue and study pictures of older people, paying special attention to the age spots and other aspects of their complexions. These can (and should) be simulated with makeup. Disguising the jaw line can be accomplished as described at right.

eye liner takes considerable practice for most people. Almost everyone uses the free hand as some sort of stabilizer for the brush hand, and many use a fingertip to keep the eye closed when applying color to the upper lid.

Forehead: The worst thing you can do to your forehead is try to paint wrinkles on it. No matter how careful you are, the result will probably be a forehead that looks as if a truck ran over it! To give an impression of age, simply highlight the frontal eminence and the superciliary arch. This will increase the apparent depth of the slight depression between the two. Don't put a shadow between the two highlights or you will

NO EXCEPTIONS!

There is only one rule I can think of that has no exceptions, and it applies to theatrical makeup:

NEVER PUT ON A SHADOW WITHOUT A HIGHLIGHT.

There are plenty of times when a highlight is applied without a shadow, but the reverse never happens!

look like you have a dirty forehead. As a special note mostly for men, applying highlight at the hairline, well up on the frontal eminence, gives the effect of a receding hairline.

Jowls: One of the muscles that loses tone and sags with age is the small muscle just below and outside the mouth on the jaw line. To give this effect, you must first find the muscle by placing a finger on your chin and your thumb about half way along your mandible, then squeezing gently. This will usually cause a crease to appear at the front edge of the muscle. Mark the location of this crease with a little shadow color, well down on the mandible. From this point, draw a semicircular line extending below the jaw line, toward the back, and up again onto the mandible. (You may also wish to add a shadow line under the chin, connecting the inner ends of the two original creases. This is especially useful in the portrayal of a double chin.) Apply a soft highlight within the semicircle, making sure it crosses below the jaw line. For a double chin, apply a soft highlight below the shadow under your chin. For a fatter character, you may also want to extend the original shadow lines farther back under the jaw line before crossing above the mandible.

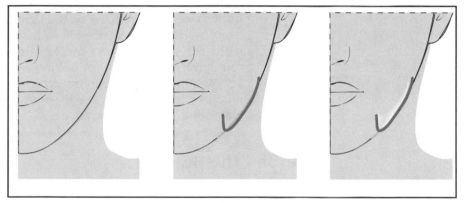

Hollow Cheeks: Giving the appearance of hollow cheeks is mostly a matter of finding the correct spot to apply the shadow color. The shadow should be applied along the line of the zygomatic arch, just where it begins to curve down and in toward the upper gums and teeth. Shadow color applied too low looks like dirty cheeks. The shadow must be carefully applied along the cheekbone, then pulled down onto the cheek with the flat of the brush. Leave the top edge of the shadow fairly well defined, but not as sharp as you would for a wrinkle. Apply highlight color above the shadow, pulling it slightly upward. Be careful not to let the two colors touch or mix.

Temporal Fossæ: With age, the temples tend to become more pronounced. Apply shadow color in a line just outside the ridge that defines the fossa, beginning near the eyebrow and extending to the hair line. Blend the shadow down and out into the fossa itself. Soften the front edge of the shadow slightly, increasing the softness as the shadow approaches the hairline, reflecting the flattening out of the ridge of bone. Apply your highlight directly on the ridge, pulling it slightly in toward the center of the forehead.

129

Powder: Powder must be applied over creme-type makeup to set it and take away the shine. It's the final step in the makeup process, since it is extremely difficult to apply and blend additional makeup over the powder. The best applicator for powder is one of those big, soft, round brushes (sprinkle powder on the brush — or dip the brush into the powder — then lightly whisk it onto the face), but the traditional powder puff will work, too. Just remember: *pat* the powder onto your face — rubbing with the puff will scrub makeup off your face, ruining the makeup and the powder puff. In either case, be sure to lean forward so that powder won't drop onto your clothes.

How Strong?

How much makeup should you apply? And how strong should it be? The only way to tell for sure is to make your best guess, then try it out by standing on the stage, under the lighting to be used for your performance. Have the director — or somebody else with a good eye — look at you from various distances from the stage. Things being what they are, your makeup will most likely appear a bit too strong from the front rows and perhaps a bit too faint from the back rows, when it is just right for most of the house. And remember, when you're looking at yourself in the makeup mirror, you're much closer to your face than any member of the audience will be!

Beyond the Basics

There's lots more to know about makeup, of course. How to use crepe hair for beards and moustaches, nose putty and other materials for changing the actual shape of the nose, making older actors look younger, and so on. Television and movie makeup, where the camera (and audience) move very close to the actor, sometimes requires making a plaster cast of the actor's face and producing latex pieces to be adhered to the skin before "paint" makeup is applied.

These and other techniques are explained in any of several books about makeup. If you're interested in going beyond the basics, check your library and local bookstores for these books and keep learning!

Exercises:

1. Begin a makeup morgue of your own. The best pictures — color or black and white — come from magazines. Be sure you have permission before you clip them! Use rubber cement to mount your pictures on heavy paper such as biology or botany paper. Organization is important: your collection will grow, and you'll want to be able to find things as easily as possible! Remember, too, that you're making a morgue, not a collage, so keep the pictures on each page well spaced. Keep your morgue pages in a three ring binder.

2. Complete the lab sequence in this chapter.

3. Plan and execute the makeup for a character from a play. Include a complete character analysis and makeup drawing. Specify the materials you intend to use. Complete the project by applying the makeup as for a performance on your own school's stage.

CHAPTER FOURTEEN

DIRECTING FOR THE STAGE

What does a director do? Everything! The director guides every aspect of a production: actors, scenery, costumes, lighting — you name it. The director is responsible for defining and achieving the specific artistic goal of the production.

Although the director may not build or paint any scenery or sew any costumes or hang any lights, he or she is responsible for coordinating the activities of all those who do. While the director may not go on-stage and perform for the audience, he or she is responsible for planning and rehearsing the actions of those who do. In short, the director is the unifying force behind a play production, the one who makes sure that all the pieces fit.

Becoming a good director is a lifelong process. It involves knowing as much as possible about as many things as you can — not only things theatrical but things in general. The more you know about everything, the more you bring to the challenging and rewarding task of directing a play. History, music, psychology, literature, science, philosophy, art, math, woodworking, dance — knowledge in all these areas and others will add to your effectiveness as a director. As a matter of fact, such knowledge will help you in almost anything you do in life: the more you know about people, the world, and the universe, the more possibilities you will be able to see.

Because this book is intended for students of theatre, we'll confine our discussion to the specifics of the process of working with actors: interpreting the script, planning the action, and conducting rehearsals. Understanding these three topics will get you started as a director.

Interpreting the Script

The director must begin with a thorough understanding of the script. To this end, I suggest reading the entire script at least three times. First, read the script as if you were an audience member — just to get a basic idea of the plot, characters, and mood. Second, read the entire script again, this time paying particular attention to what each scene is about (see Chapter 7) and how this action is revealed through the dialog and movements of the characters. Third, read the script with a pencil in your hand — ready to take notes, underline important passages, draw little diagrams in the margin.

First Reading

Read the script all the way through in one sitting, just as if you were a member of the audience watching the play. You can even take a short break at intermissions! Be sure to read everything, as suggested in Chapter 7; that way you won't miss important details of the action that are given in the stage directions. By the time you have finished the reading, you will know the basics: plot, character, and theme. Take a few minutes to write down your impressions of the play at this point, including both "What happens in the play?" and "What is this play about?"

Second Reading

This time there are no surprises. You already know the outcome of the plot, the identities of the characters, and so on. As you read, use a pencil to divide the script into small, workable sections.

Plays with many characters and/or many scenes can often be divided into "French scenes." A French scene includes the dialog and action that take place between any two characters, ending (and beginning the next French scene) when a new character enters and/or one of the characters exits. Stay flexible! The particular script you're working with may better use scenes of three or four characters, or any convenient number. Sometimes it's impossible to decide the exact moment when one French scene ends and the next begins, but scheduling rehearsals for a show with many characters is often easier — and rehearsal time is used more efficiently — using this method.

You need to list the characters in the play. Write a brief description for each character in the play. For each character, decide on an overall motivation in the play — what does this character want to *do*?

Third Reading

This time, read through the script with a pencil and paper handy, ready to take notes and make lists as you pay attention to the mechanics of the play. Jot down casting issues such as the number of characters. How many male? How many female? Are there special casting requirements (one of the characters must play the guitar, one of the characters is a six-year-old child)? Write down set design issues such as the number of settings and the maximum number of characters on-stage at the same time in each setting. Do they all have to sit down at the same time? Are there special requirements for costumes, props, lighting, sound effects?

Beginning directors seldom have the luxury of working with a full staff of designers, so you'll probably need to do your own set design. Begin by listing the specific requirements of the set: doors, windows, seating arrangements, etc. Then make several pencil sketches of possible floor plans. Be sure you take into account the sight lines of the theatre — don't place furniture or other scenic units so that they will mask large sections of the stage from many seats in the house. Also, keep in mind the traffic patterns: when the actors are moving around the stage, will they run into each other? Will their movements create visually interesting patterns? If you're doing a realistic play, make sure the entire set, including the off-stage "rooms," is architecturally possible — don't put a window right between the door to the bedroom and the door to the kitchen!

When you've considered all your sketches and made your decision, make a final copy of the floor plan. It's not absolutely necessary to draw everything to exact scale, but try to keep sizes and distances at least approximately correct.

Planning the Action

Blocking the play, planning the action, is a time-consuming job that forces the director to come to grips with his or her artistic vision of the play. Here are some of the things you need to consider.

Composition

The director must consider that the audience will be seeing the play as a series of pictures. Even though there may be almost constant movement on the stage, you should keep in mind the requirements for pleasing visual compositions. Possibly the most important element is *balance*. The set itself should be "in balance," and the arrangement of actors on the stage should be in balance, too.

It's important to remember that balance does not mean absolute symmetry — things on one side of the stage don't have to be exactly matched by things on the other side. Imagine that the stage is a see-saw or teeter-totter, balanced at center stage. Items that are visually heavy (such as large or dark pieces of furniture) are easier to balance if they are closer to the center of the stage. Actors and groups of actors are "objects," too.

In the final analysis, the best guideline is this: use your eyes. If the "stage picture"

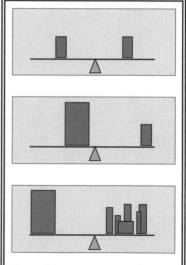

Top diagram: symmetrical balance. Middle diagram: large object near center balanced by smaller object farther from center. Bottom diagram: large object far from center balanced by many smaller objects.

looks good to you, then the composition is probably okay. (Of course, I can't let this opportunity pass by without mentioning that the study of art, both studio art — painting, drawing, sculpture — and art history, provides invaluable training of your artistic, æsthetic eye.)

Picturization

Directing a play is like an extended and expanded form of storytelling. While most of the story is contained in the dialog, the director must use every tool at his disposal — including the stage picture — to help tell the story. Think about it this way: radio drama depends entirely on what the audience can *hear*, movies and television plays depend largely on what the audience can *see* (that's why there are so often long sequences without any dialog at all), stage plays combine the seeing and the hearing — with an emphasis but not a total dependence on the hearing.

What the audience can see must help tell the story of the play. Imagine that you are watching television with the sound turned off. Most of the time you can keep up with at least the general outline of the story: man holds gun through teller cage in bank, teller stuffs money in bag, man takes bag to door, man shoots bank guard, and so on. Although most people can't turn the sound off when they see a play, you must plan the action so that *if they could,* they could still understand the basic outlines of the story.

What the director must do is translate the words of the script and the intentions of the characters into pictures. These pictures don't stand still, so patterns of movement are important. Here are some basic patterns of movement that are often used to express the dynamics of a relationship on-stage. In the first, character A "attacks" character B, who stands firm. The attack need not be physical, of course, so long as character A is trying to persuade character B of something. Sometimes, character B "runs away" from character A's attack. This movement pattern is used in everything from chasing one another across the stage in a farce, to stalking a victim in a melodrama, to the slow, romantic pursuit of the beautiful girl by the handsome hero in a romance. A third possibility is that character B responds in kind, staging a counterattack. This pattern is often used in arguments and fight scenes. In a scene in which character A meets resistance from character B and decides to keep trying different tactics of persuasion, as when a teenager tries to persuade Dad

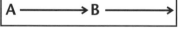

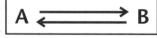

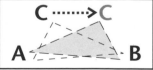

to part with the family car for the evening, can be expressed visually with yet another movement pattern. One final pattern that you should know involves three (or more) characters. Very often, the conflict in a scene involves a third character who "takes sides" with either A or B. If character C's allegiance changes during the scene, you might suggest this by using a pattern of shifting triangles.

Psychology

These few notes certainly won't replace an introductory course in psychology, nor even a few years of living and watching people. They will provide a starting point for your blocking, especially in terms of picturization.

Most people who haven't given it a great deal of thought would probably say that *love* and *hate* are opposites. It's worth considering, however, that love and hate — or any strong emotion — have a great deal in common. In fact, the opposite of both *love* and *hate* is *indifference*. This is important for the director because it reveals movement patterns in the script.

Think of love and hate as the poles of a horseshoe magnet. The strength of the magnetic attraction is strongest at the poles of the magnet, and grows weaker as you move away from the pole. The center of the magnet attracts not at all. In the same way, both *love* and *hate* attract while *indifference* has no attractive effect.

It seems obvious that two characters who love each other will tend to move toward each other onstage. It is perhaps less obvious, but equally true, that characters who hate each other are drawn together. If the two lovers are left alone, their attraction might end in an embrace, while the two haters might come to blows. The director often allows both kinds of characters to come together on the stage. Placing an obstacle between the two haters, whether it be another person, a piece of furniture, or something else, prevents the characters from actually coming to blows.

The setting can be used to reveal character psychology in many plays because it determines where on the stage each character spends most of his or her time. This "home base" theory works well, for example, in a play about a family, set in the family's living room. Does Dad have a favorite easy chair? Does Mom sit at the end of the sofa beside the lamp? Does Junior have a special place to sit and do his homework? Many real-life families use their homes in just this fashion, and similar ideas will often work in other kinds of plays.

137

Gaining Emphasis

Sometimes it seems that the director of a movie or television show has it easy. If it's important that the audience see the expression on a certain character's face at a certain moment, all the director need do is take a close-up of the facial reaction. The audience has no choice but to look at that face at that moment.

For the stage director, life isn't so simple. Unless you're directing a non-realistic play in which all the lights can be turned off except a single tight spot on the actor's face, you can't force the audience to look at anything. Their eyes have the freedom to roam the entire stage. You must use much more subtle techniques to make sure the audience sees what you want it to see.

Each of the following techniques for gaining emphasis will direct the audience's eyes and attention to a particular actor or group of actors. Each is described separately, but remember that a play is a moving, dynamic process, and sometimes it's difficult to isolate just one technique at a time. Once again, it's important to use your own eyes and ears to check on the success of your work!

DIRECTING WHAT?

Most people think of the director's job as "directing *actors*" around the stage. Those with more theater knowledge might add *designers*, *technicians*, and *stagehands* to the list. Many directors, though, find it helpful to think of their job as "directing *the audience's attention*." After all, entertaining and enlightening the audience is what theater is all about, and if we can't get the audience to see/hear and notice the important expressions, actions, and lines then we will most likely fail to either entertain or enlighten!

Movement: The human eye is attracted by movement. That's why it's generally considered bad form for an actor to move while another actor is saying a line. A strong movement by an actor will attract the attention of the audience almost immediately, almost no matter what else is happening on the stage. So, for example, if it's important that the audience see *Mary's* reaction to *Frank's* line, make sure that the actor playing Frank stands still after the line, while the actor playing Mary turns, or takes a step, or sits down, or stands up suddenly, even if Mary doesn't have a line to say.

Height: Other things being equal, the audience will tend to look at actors who are taller or otherwise higher above the floor of the stage. An actor who is standing gains more attention than an actor who is sitting down. An actor standing on a raised part of the set such as a stair landing gains emphasis compared to an actor standing at ground level.

Body Position: Actors facing the audience, in a full front position, will gain the attention of the audience. One-quarter position is next strongest.

Profile still has some strength, but three-quarter position is weaker than full back.

Stage Location: Some areas of the stage are "stronger" than others. Perhaps because English — and most other languages — are written and read from left-to-right and top-to-bottom, the Up Right area (corresponding to the upper left-hand corner, from the audience's point of view) is perhaps stronger than Up Left or even Down Left. Of course, ask any actor what's the "best" place to stand and the answer will almost surely be, "Center Stage!"

Sound: Other things being equal, the audience will look at the actor who is speaking (or making another sound) instead of one who is quiet. This is especially important in a tense scene where a pause is needed between lines. The actor making the pause must "pick up the cue" so that the audience knows where to look, and one way to do this is by making a sound, or saying just the first word or two of the line *before* pausing.

Light: Many plays, even those that are called realistic, will nevertheless allow some "fiddling" with the brightness of the lighting. Even if the difference is so slight as to be scarcely noticeable, the audience will pay more attention to an actor in a light slightly brighter than that shining on the rest of the stage.

> ## Where's the Door?
> Body position and stage location considerations often influence the design of the set! Many sets have at least one entrance door. Should the door be placed in a side wall or the back wall of the set? Study the script to determine if there are entrances or exits that are important pieces of business in themselves, or are accompanied by important lines of dialog. Generally speaking, an actor makes a stronger exit through a door in the side wall — he doesn't have to turn his back to the audience. Entrances, however, are strongest when made through an upstage wall — the actor is facing the audience immediately.

Line of Sight: This is a very useful and subtle tool for the director. When an audience member looks at several actors on the stage, his or her eye doesn't see everything at the same time. Other things being equal, our eyes tend to begin at the "top left-hand corner" and work their way across the stage and down. When our eyes are stopped momentarily by seeing an actor, we almost invariably look at his or her face. If the actor is looking at another actor, we tend to follow the direction of his or her gaze, and we find ourselves looking at the same other actor. Careful use of this technique will allow the director to focus the audience on a single actor without having to have all the other actors stare directly at him.

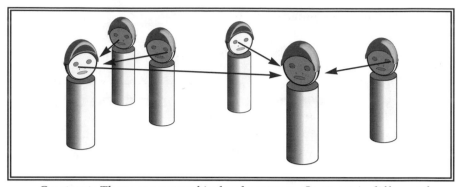

Contrast: There are many kinds of contrast. Contrast is different from the previously discussed techniques because it doesn't depend on "other things being equal." As a matter of fact it's just the opposite, depending on things being different. The audience will tend to pay more attention to whatever on the stage is different — in any respect — from other things or people on the stage. If ten actors are wearing blue suits, then one actor wearing a brown suit will attract the attention of the audience. If six actors are standing, then a seated actor will draw the attention, unless the standing actors are hiding him from the audience. If all but one of the actors are moving around, the stationary actor will become the focal point for the audience. Here are some graphic examples of contrast. Size, shape, color, position, light, movement, even sound — all these can be used to provide attention-grabbing contrast.

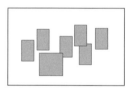 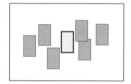 

Scheduling Rehearsals

So many factors influence the rehearsal schedule (length of the script, number of days available, amount of time available each day, experience level of the cast and crew) that making a schedule for a specific play must be done by the director of the play at the time of the production.

That said, here's what a rehearsal schedule should include. The percentages in the right-hand column are the suggested allocation of your rehearsal time. Adapt freely to suit your specific needs.

Read-through

Blocking and review rehearsals   20%

Working rehearsals   25%

Run-through of complete script
Cast goes off book no later than half way
    through the rehearsal period
Off-book rehearsals   5% – 10%
Run-through complete script
Polishing rehearsals   25% – 30%
Run-through complete script
Technical rehearsals   5%
Dress rehearsals   5%

Many directors find it convenient to build the rehearsal schedule backwards, starting with the performance dates, then final dress rehearsal, and so on back to the first reading. Specific information about each kind of rehearsal is given later in this chapter, under the heading, *Conducting Rehearsals*.

Preparing the Prompt Book

The director's copy of the script is often called a prompt book, because it or a similarly prepared copy is used for prompting actors at rehearsals after they have gone "off book." In the days before photocopy machines, a prompt book was made by cutting the script apart into separate pages and then gluing them onto three-hole punched heavy paper with a rectangular hole — slightly smaller than the script page — in the middle. This method gave each page of the script a very wide margin in which the director could write down blocking, character notes, light cues, and so on. A photocopy machine allows today's director to achieve a similar effect without all the cutting and pasting.

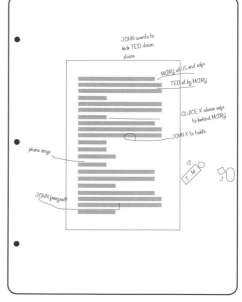

A prompt book is indispensable. It gives you plenty of room for writing and drawing small diagrams to remind yourself of important character relationships, movement patterns, seating arrangements, etc. A carefully prepared prompt book is a great time-saver at rehearsal, and it helps persuade the cast (and crew) that you are serious about this directing project.

Many directors still use a time-honored (or clichéd, if you prefer) method of blocking a play. They sit at the kitchen or dining room table, define a small area as the stage, and use the salt shaker, pepper shaker, and other tabletop "stuff" to represent actors, moving them around the table-stage as they work their way through the play. This is an excellent system because it uses real objects to aid in your visualization of the play. It makes it easier to plan for good composition and picturization, and avoids traffic jams at rehearsal. Other directors draw tons of little sketches, most of which are thrown away. Other directors have developed their own techniques for visualizing and recording what they "see" happening on the stage. You will develop your own method, but for now, try the "salt and pepper" method of blocking the script.

Be sure you write all your notes in pencil. Directors always change their minds about blocking and other things, and erasing is neater than crossing out!

If all this seems like a lot of trouble, remember that every hour you spend preparing your prompt book will save

> ## UNSOLICITED SUBMISSIONS
>
> **Don't be afraid to listen to suggestions from your actors, and give them serious consideration. You don't need to agree automatically with every idea, but you shouldn't reject them out of hand. Being open to discussions of this sort will not weaken your authority with the cast, but will likely increase it. Besides, after the first week or so of rehearsal, each actor probably knows more about his or her individual character than you do!**

you and your actors at least two hours at rehearsal. Rehearsal time is too valuable to waste, and actors get tired of standing around while the director tries to figure out what to do next. Changes in your blocking are inevitable once you see the actors on the stage. Time and energy spent in carefully working out the blocking in advance, though, will help avoid time-consuming mistakes such as having to take the entire cast back two pages to change the blocking because there are three people standing in front of the door when the main character is supposed to enter!

It's a good idea for the prompt book to include copies of all light plots, costume plots, prop lists, rehearsal schedules, and anything else that is important to the success of the show. The stage manager should be collecting the same information from designers and crew heads, but better safe than sorry. If the light crew head becomes ill, the written light cue sheets, light plot, instrument schedule, and so on will enable a replacement crew head to carry on with minimal effort. If the stage manager loses his or her prompt book, the director's book is a resource more valuable than gold. And if the director is unable to attend rehearsal, the prompt book allows the stage manager, cast, and crews to continue working rather than wasting a rehearsal.

Conducting Rehearsals

There are three rules for good rehearsals:

1. Don't waste time.

2. Don't waste time.

3. Don't waste time.

In other words, don't waste time! At rehearsal, the cast and crew depend on you for direction. That's why preparation is so important. If you spend three hours preparing for a one-hour rehearsal, you will be saving time for everybody at rehearsal. If you're working with five actors and four crew members, it takes only twenty minutes of *clock* time to equal three hours of *people* time (9 x 20 = 180 minutes = 3 hours).

Read-Through

The first rehearsal is often a sit-down affair — but dinner is not served! The director (and usually the stage manager) lead the cast in reading aloud the entire script. This is an opportunity to clarify pronunciation and meaning of unusual words, and to discuss the director's basic concept for the play.

The director should be prepared to tell the cast what's important about the play. This includes the date of the play, the location of its setting, and its type and/or style. In many cases it also includes information about the playwright and his or her place in theatre history. Don't be afraid of generating questions from the cast that you can't answer! Simply note the question and find the answer in time for the next rehearsal.

Blocking and Review Rehearsals

Blocking rehearsals are slow. Each actor must be given his or her movements, and be given time to write the movements in his or her script. You must often struggle with the cast's natural tendency to create a "normal" speed and flow. Allowing them to go too fast will probably mean they don't take the time to write down the blocking. It may seem to save time, but will result in wasted time when you must give them the blocking again at the next rehearsal.

After each scene or act is blocked, either the same day or the next rehearsal, allow the actors to go through it again. This gives them a sense of the flow of the scene, and gives you a chance to see problems in the blocking and make changes or corrections.

Working Rehearsals

These intensive rehearsals should be used by the actors for characterization and by the director for emphasizing important structural elements of the play. Actors should be encouraged to experiment with body and voice, trying different walks and talks, to make their characters come alive. The director should point out important plot points (such as crisis and climax), character relationships, and the importance of these to the overall effect of the production.

The cast will be working with scripts in hand, but they should be encouraged to get their eyes off the pages as soon as possible. The stage manager should sit with the prompt book to call cues ("Lights up," "Ring...ring...ring...," etc.) and read the lines of absent actors. The director must be free to watch and listen to the actors; if you don't know how the play is going now, you won't be able to guide it appropriately.

These rehearsals are often very choppy. Sometimes a page or two will be repeated several times. Sometimes many minutes will be spent working on just a few lines of dialog or a small piece of business. It's important, though, to make

---

SPLIT REHEARSALS

Here's a good way to make sure you rehearse *all* the play as often as possible. Number the pages of the prompt book in reverse, beginning with the last page. Write the number in the upper right hand corner of the page. At a working or polishing rehearsal, have your stage manager keep tabs on the time remaining. When the number of minutes remaining equals the number of pages left in the script, allow the cast to run the play without stopping. At the next rehearsal, allow the cast to run without stopping until you reach the page where you stopped "working" yesterday. Continue working (slowing down) from this point until the minutes remaining equal the pages remaining, then run through to the end.

If your rehearsals are short, you may want to reverse-number each Act of the play separately, insuring that an entire Act is "done" every day.

---

sure that no section of the script is slighted, and that you don't allow too much time to elapse between the rehearsals of a given scene. For example, if you schedule three rehearsals to work each act, there will be eight or nine days between rehearsals for a given act. Avoid this problem by scheduling a "run-through" of Act III between the working sessions for Acts I and II, and a run-through of Act I between working sessions for Acts II and III.

Off-Book Rehearsals

About halfway through your rehearsal schedule, the play will begin to look and sound like a real play! But disaster is about to strike: the cast members have to go off book. Suddenly, the wonderful timing, the flow of a scene, the lively interplay between characters, all disappear. The actors can scarcely think beyond, "What do I say next?"

Some beginning directors take pity on their actors, allowing them "a few extra rehearsals" before making them leave their scripts off-stage. But at this stage of rehearsal, a script is as much a crutch for an actor as a real crutch is to a person recovering from a broken leg. If you delay getting rid of the crutch, you only delay the strengthening of the leg (or the play). The terrible "falling apart" of the play is inevitable — it will happen no matter how long you wait to get rid of the scripts. And the longer you wait, the less time you leave for your actors to recover from the disaster and go on to build a strong and polished performance.

Don't expect too much of your actors at this kind of rehearsal. It's probably pointless to stop the rehearsal to add a new bit of business or work on the timing of a scene. The important thing is that you be firm but supportive. Insist that your actors maintain concentration, calling "Line" without any words and without looking at the prompter.

The worst effects of going off book will disappear within two or three rehearsals. Everybody can heave a big sigh of relief and get on with the polishing of the play.

Polishing Rehearsals

Freed of their scripts, your actors find themselves capable of new levels of creativity. These rehearsals are similar to the earlier working rehearsals. Individual scenes, individual pages, individual lines can be gone over and polished until they shine. As before, remember to keep the entire play "current" by scheduling regular run-throughs and/or by using the split rehearsal technique.

Watch the rehearsal from different parts of the house. Make sure you can see and hear the actors no matter where you sit. You can still make changes in the blocking if they are needed.

The last polishing rehearsals should be done without a prompter. Allow the cast to run at least an entire Act without stopping. Take notes of problems (line readings, slow cue pick-ups, low energy levels, etc.) to give to the actors after the rehearsal. Be sure to note their improvements, too!

Technical Rehearsals

These rehearsals mark the end of working with the actors on the fine points of their performances. No changes should be made in the blocking, and the actors should stop experimenting, working for consistency rather than invention.

Lights, sound effects, all props and scenery should be complete and are integrated into the play at rehearsal. This usually means you'll have to stop the actors to adjust lighting levels or sound volume, and repeat sections of the script for the benefit of the light crew and sound crew.

Because tech rehearsals are so stressful, many directors prefer to integrate sound, lights, and so on as they are ready, earlier in the rehearsal process. If your working space, time available, and crew experience level permit it, this method is highly recommended.

You'll be taking notes, now, for lights, sound, props, shifting, and cast. Allow time at the end of rehearsal for giving notes as well as cleaning up, putting away props, and so on.

> # THE DIRECTOR'S ROLES
>
> A director has to wear many different hats. Here's a *partial* list!
>
> ### ACTING TEACHER
> ### PERSONAL COUNSELOR
> ### STAGEHAND
> ### CHEERLEADER
> ### CRITIC
> ### DESIGNER
> ### PUBLIC RELATIONS EXPERT
> ### DISCIPLINARIAN
> ### COMEDIAN
> ### ADVERTISING EXECUTIVE
> ### ACTOR
> ### FAN

Dress Rehearsals

Dress rehearsals are like performances without an audience. The play is performed without stopping — unless something drastic happens...the lights won't go on for the beginning of Act II, the stage right wall collapses, etc.

Time permitting, it's a good idea to allow the actors at least two dress rehearsals without makeup. This allows them to become familiar with the feel of wearing their costumes and practice any changes — without getting any makeup on the clothes. There should be at least two rehearsals with full makeup, including the final dress rehearsal, which should be as much like a performance as you can manage, right down to the time of the opening curtain. Some directors like to have an invited audience at the final dress rehearsal, giving the cast and crew a chance to experience audience response and reaction before the first "real" performance.

Your notes at dress rehearsals will include every aspect of the show. Allow plenty of time for giving notes to cast and crew, as well as time for the cast to put away their costumes and remove their stage makeup.

Performance

At last it's opening night! What do you say to the cast before the curtain rises? Most directors — at least in amateur theatre — remind their casts of all the hard work they've put in, encourage them to "play it the way we rehearsed it," and tell them how wonderful they are.

In the professional theatre, the director's job is done on opening night. The play "belongs" to the stage manager from now on. Amateur directors, though, should continue to exert control over their cast and crew. Help avoid the "second night slump" by building up the energy level. Remind the cast and crew that every audience, even on closing night, deserves their best efforts, and that clowning around or playing tricks on each other is *not* appropriate.

Directing is as rewarding as it is frustrating. There's no thrill quite like putting together a winning performance. Enjoy!

Exercises:

1. Write a report that tells of the development of play directing, from the actor/managers of Elizabethan days, to the *regisseurs* of nineteenth-century Europe, to the art of directing as we know it today.

2. Read and report on a biography or autobiography of one of the great twentieth-century stage directors.

3. Prepare a prompt book, including set sketches and blocking, for a one-act play.

CHAPTER FIFTEEN

SCENE DESIGN AND PAINTING

Designing scenery for the stage is a creative challenge that offers immense artistic and emotional rewards to those who pursue it with dedication. Actors, directors, costumers, lighting designers — anybody connected with the performing arts — will benefit from learning the basics of set design and scene painting. Many people put these ideas to work in their own homes, too.

Many professional set designers are painters. They begin the design process by drawing thumbnail sketches, developing their ideas from a vision of what the set will look like from the audience. These designers use watercolors, acrylics, or other media to produce wonderful paintings — called *renderings* — of their final designs.

Most of us don't have that kind of skill in painting, but we can still become competent designers. By focusing our attention first on the groundplan — the arrangement of furniture, doors, and other set pieces — we can provide a design that works well for the directors and actors, helping them to communicate the playwright's message to the audience.

> **REALITY CHECK**
>
> **Most of the plays done in schools use fairly limited scenery: a single interior, a unit set with platforms and curtains, etc. While this chapter will give you the basics for any set design, the focus will be on the practical aspects of school theatre set design and painting.**

Reading the Script

No matter which approach we take, the design process begins with reading the script. Most people find that three readings are helpful.

The First Reading

Read the script all the way through — preferably at one sitting. This reading will give you basic information about the script and a general feeling for the play: the plot, the characters, the historical setting, the mood, type and style of the play. It's almost the same as the information and feeling the audience would get upon seeing a performance of the play for the first time.

The Second Reading

As you go through the script again, your focus will move away from the broad strokes of plot and character and mood. Since you already know what happens in the story, you'll be able to concentrate on the structure of the play.

Exposition, inciting incident, crisis, climax, denouement — all the terms discussed in Chapter 7 — will be easier to identify. You'll also be better able to determine the theme of the play, and see how the various elements work together.

The Third Reading

For the third reading, equip yourself with pencil and paper. You'll need to take specific notes as you read. Pay particular attention in this reading to any information provided in the dialog or stage directions that directly relates to the setting.

How many entrances/exits are required? Are they plain doors, French doors, secret panels, curtained arches? When characters leave the stage, where do they go — the hall, a bedroom, the kitchen, outdoors, elsewhere?

How many people must be seated all at one time? You will have to provide chairs, sofas, benches, window seats, stools, or even floor space enough for all of them.

Does the action *require* a fireplace or stove? Or does the dialog specifically forbid such a thing? Are there practical light fixtures on the stage? Is there a telephone, a radio, a television, or a washing machine on the stage?

Is it necessary to have all or part of the staircase (if there is one) visible to the audience? If there are windows, are we to see the actors passing by "outside" the room as they enter or exit? What else must the audience see through the windows?

Are there clues in the dialog or action about the decor of the room? Is it important that the floor be covered with an Oriental rug? Do we need a wall safe behind a picture?

Plays vary so widely that it's impossible to list here all the possibilities.

> ### SOUND FAMILIAR?
>
> "Hmmm...," you're saying to yourself. "Seems like I've read something about this before." You are absolutely correct, if you have read Chapter 14, *Directing for the Stage.* And if you haven't read it yet, be sure you do read it before you go much farther in your efforts to learn about scene design. The director and designer must work closely together (even if they aren't one and the same person!) and the work of each depends on the work of the other. A shared outlook and understanding are vital.

Suffice it to say that you must concentrate as you read, keeping your mind open and your pencil poised!

Basic Sketching and Drafting

Designing for the theatre used to require skills in basic pencil and paper drafting: using a drawing board, T-square, and triangles. The computer age has brought a new ease to designers, allowing the experienced computer user to try several ideas without starting all over or erasing large numbers of lines. Basic drafting techniques are still used, and they have influenced the look of groundplans and other design drawings even in the computer age. The ability to read as well as draw pencil sketches and rough groundplans — even finished plans when no computer is available — is vitally important.

The Groundplan

In architecture and interior design, they are called floor plans. In the theatre, they're called groundplans. Whatever they're called, they are "bird's-eye views" or maps of the stage. They show the size and placement of objects on the stage. Here's a sample groundplan.

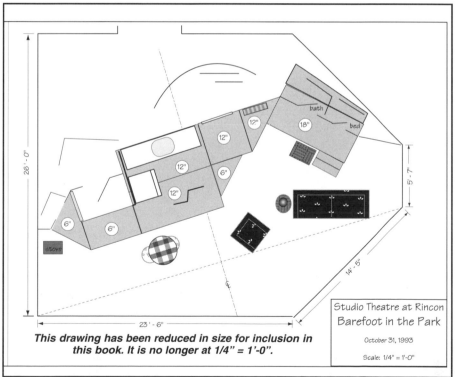

This drawing has been reduced in size for inclusion in this book. It is no longer at 1/4" = 1'-0".

Studio Theatre at Rincon
Barefoot in the Park
October 31, 1993
Scale: 1/4" = 1'-0"

A finished groundplan is drawn to scale, that is each inch on the drawing represents a definite and consistent larger distance on the actual stage. Large scale drawings often use a scale where ½ inch on the drawing equals one foot of space on the stage. Many schools use a smaller scale, say ¼ inch equals one foot, because it allows the entire stage to be shown on a standard 8½ x 11 sheet of paper.

Preliminary groundplans can be more like sketches. They needn't be drawn exactly to scale, but you do need to be reasonably consistent in your dimensions so that a chair doesn't appear to be larger than a sofa, for example.

What does a chair look like on a groundplan? How about a table, or a door, or a window? Remember, a groundplan is a top view — you show only what you can see when you look down on the object in question — so you can't see the legs of chairs or tables. Here are some of the standard symbols used on groundplans.

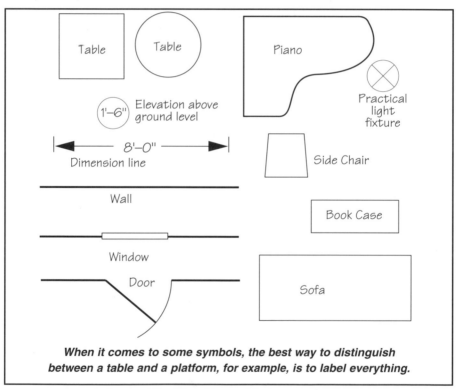

When it comes to some symbols, the best way to distinguish between a table and a platform, for example, is to label everything.

As you can see, the symbols are simple line drawings, not difficult or complicated to produce with a pencil and eraser. Note the importance of labeling the various items in the groundplan. You can draw a circle on top of a rectangle and clarify everything by labeling them **telephone** and **table**.

A ruler is necessary. A triangle (for drawing angles) and a compass (for

152

drawing circles and arcs) are handy, but other items can be used in a pinch. Look around and improvise! A CD case can be used to draw a right angle. Various coins, cups, and glasses can serve as guides for circles.

A steel tape measure, or at the very least a yardstick, is also a requirement. How long is a couch? How far from the front of a chair to the back of a chair? How much room does an actor need to walk between the back of the sofa and a wall? You'll need to know the exact size of the objects in your drawings, as well as the dimensions of your stage or other performing area. Being precise in your measurements is vitally important if you are designing scenery that will be built or assembled and painted specifically for your show, but it's also important if you're doing a small scene for which the basic questions are simpler ones such as "Where is the door?" and "How is the furniture arranged?"

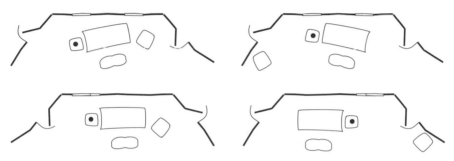

Sketching

Many people protest loudly that they "can't draw." Well, few of us are in any immediate danger of having our work exhibited at the National Gallery, but that doesn't mean we can't communicate with a pencil! With a little practice, almost everybody can learn to sketch something on paper to show another person what kind of chair is needed for a particular scene, or how the window should look. In short, you don't need to be an artist. All you need is a pencil, some paper, some motivation, and a little practice.

Groundplans usually start life as rough sketches, too. The designer puts his or her first ideas on paper quickly, then revises, changes, tries other ideas. When one of the ideas finally "clicks," it's time for the ruler, triangles, and compass.

Creating Alternative Ideas

Creativity — in this case, good design — is most often the result of hard work, knowledge, and persistence, not good luck or inspiration. Here's an example.

One of the pitfalls that a designer (or any other creative person) can fall into is the "my first idea is the only idea" trap. This is an easy trap to fall into, because one idea often masks the possibility of other ideas. If you read in the script that the front door of the living room is at stage left, you will most likely find it difficult to generate any design ideas that put the front door anywhere else. Even if the idea for putting the front door at stage left is your very own, if it comes to you in a blinding flash of white-hot inspiration, *that doesn't mean that it's the best idea!* Unless you have at least two ideas, you have no way to decide if one is better than another. By generating alternatives, you give yourself the opportunity to choose. Two heads are better than one, and two ideas are better than one (and three are better than two, too!). If, after examining several alternate ideas, you decide that your first idea *is* the best idea you will benefit from choice, not depend on chance.

How can you generate alternate ideas? Sometimes it's possible to make ourselves discover new ideas or ways of looking at things by using purely "mechanical" techniques.

If your initial sketch seems to be blocking new ideas, try reversing things. Switch doors and windows from stage left to stage right. Raise lower areas up onto platforms, and lower raised areas to floor level. If you have long unbroken walls, try breaking them into shorter segments. Change from straight lines to curves. If your interior setting has three walls and two corners, try shifting to a deeper set with only two walls and one corner.

Often enough, this kind of "forced creativity" will open our eyes to possibilities we had not seen before. In the end, our design may use ideas from several of our sketches, combined in ways we would never have thought of if we had accepted our first idea as the only possible idea.

Elements of Design

Artists and designers — no matter what their field — use the following terms to talk about their work. The ideas represented by these terms become for them a part of the language of design, helping the designers to *think* about design as well as *talk* about it.

Line

A line is something you draw with a pencil. A line on a piece of paper invites the viewer's eye to travel from one end to the other. On a stage, a line does the same thing, directing the audience's eyes along a path.

On-stage, a line might be defined by the top of a wall, or the edge of a platform, or a decorative molding or chair rail. A line might also be created by an arrangement of

furniture, the way that a row of telephone poles creates a line stretching to the horizon next to the highway.

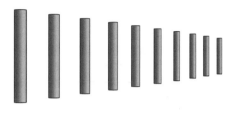

Lines can be thin or thick, straight or curved, horizontal, vertical, or diagonal. In general, straight lines are associated with drama, while curves suggest comedy or romance. Horizontal lines indicate stability; vertical lines create a feeling of grandeur and loftiness; diagonal lines signify tension.

Mass

On-stage, mass can be thought of most simply as a large object: a high platform with solid sides, a large wall, or even a "massive" piece of furniture. Visually and psychologically, mass creates a feeling of solidity and stability.

Space

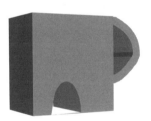

Mass occupies space. Sometimes a designer will speak of positive space and negative space. Basically, positive space is a solid object, while negative space surrounds it (and sometimes pierces it, as a tunnel through a mountain or a passage through a wall). Negative space, defined by mass (or positive space), includes the area to be occupied by the actors.

Composition and Contrast

These terms refer to vital concepts which have been discussed in Chapter 14. They apply equally well in this chapter.

Color

Dealing with color requires learning about three concepts: *hue, value,* and *intensity.* Hue is the name of the color (red, blue, green, etc.). Value is the lightness or darkness of a hue (a light value of red, accomplished by adding white paint, is pink). Intensity, also called *saturation,* is the amount of gray in the hue, which is changed by adding the complementary color (the hue directly across the color wheel).

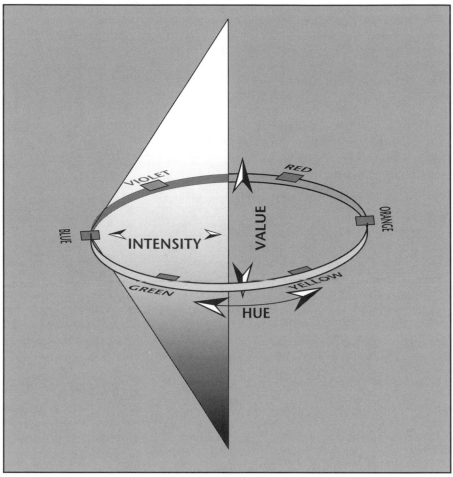

Practical Considerations

Sight lines

One of the most important things to remember in designing scenery is that different parts of the audience see the stage from different angles. Horizontal sight lines are the imaginary lines that mark the extreme view of a member of the audience sitting in the furthest left (or right) seat. Vertical sight lines mark the view from the lowest and highest seats.

Horizontal sight lines are important to the designer in planning for what the audience *must* see and what the audience *must not* see. The designer wants to be sure that all members of the audience will be able to see important objects and actors. Placing large objects downstage blocks or masks the view of actors or other objects further upstage. Here is a simplified ground-

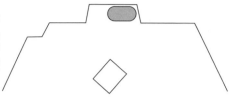

plan of a three-wall box set, with a box (or chair or table) placed down center and something else (rug? trap-door?) placed just to the left of up center.

Here's what the setting would look like from three different vantage points in the house — left, center, and right.

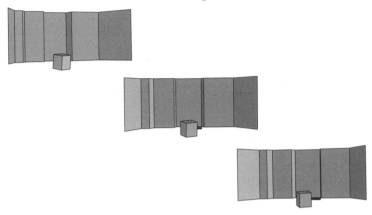

Notice that the up center object is totally invisible to people sitting house left, partially visible from house center, and almost entirely visible from house right. Let's hope that the "thing" is *not* a trap door containing the incriminating evidence, the opening of which is the climax of Act III!

Horizontal sight lines are often drawn on the finished groundplan to help the designer plan for the off-stage masking or backing (to keep the audience from seeing the prop table, the shop door, and other backstage items)

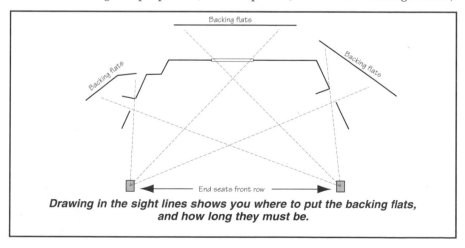

Drawing in the sight lines shows you where to put the backing flats, and how long they must be.

on the "outside" of doors and windows. Be sure your groundplan has space for the extreme left and right front row seats, then use a straight-edge to draw the sight lines.

Vertical sight lines are important, too, especially if you are designing for a proscenium theatre or a theatre with a balcony (or very steeply pitched seating area). To draw these sight lines, you'll need a different kind of drawing called a longitudinal section. This drawing shows a "slice" of the theatre from the back of the stage to the back row of seats. Identify the lowest seat and the highest seat, then draw sight lines to show the best height for borders and teasers and lights hung above the stage.

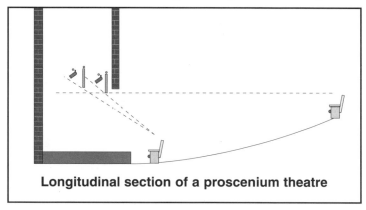

Longitudinal section of a proscenium theatre

Even if your theatre does not have a proscenium and fly gallery, it is important to consider the vertical sight lines. The height of the stage above front-row floor level and the steepness of the angle at which succeeding rows

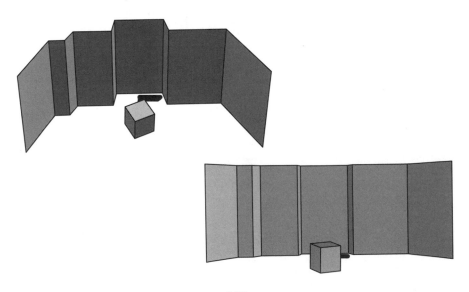

are raised (or not raised — some theatre spaces have a flat floor for the seating area) determines how much of the floor can be seen by the audience. In a theatre with high visibility of the floor, the designer will most likely want to use the floor as a strong element of the overall design. On the other hand, if the audience can't see the floor very well you may not want to spend a great deal of time or money on fancy rugs or painted groundcloths. And you may want to remind the director that the audience won't be able to see that dramatic death scene if it is played on the stage floor itself rather than on the sofa or on a platform or other raised area.

Doors Part 1

Doors in side walls of the set almost always open off-stage and upstage. That is, the knob is on the downstage side of the door, and the actor pushes the door ahead of him as he goes off the stage. In this way, the door itself (called the *shutter*) works as part of the backing. Of course, a door that serves as the entrance to the set from the "outside," a front door, must open *into* the room (unless, of course, you live in Mr. Rogers' neighborhood!).

Doors Part 2

A wall section made up of several flats will stand up without falling if it is attached to another wall section at a corner. If there is a door in the wall, though, you will have to provide extra bracing for two reasons. First, when the shutter of the door is opened its weight tends to pull the wall out of plumb. Second, when an actor closes the shutter, the wall tends to wiggle and wobble.

Off-Stage Reality

When you are laying out the groundplan for an interior setting, remember that the audience will better accept your room as "real" if your doors and windows make architectural sense. For example, don't put a window on the downstage side of a door that leads off into another room — unless the view through the window is of the other room! Take the time to think about (or even sketch) the entire apartment or house or whatever so that you'll know how the main character could exit down left into the kitchen in Act II and reappear in the same scene from the bedroom.

Thickness

Flats are less than one inch thick. Walls of modern buildings are at least four inches thick. You can't tell how thick a wall (or flat) is unless you can see a hole in the wall like a door or window or arch that reveals an edge of the wall. How do you maintain the illusion of solid walls when the audience can see the edge of a flat? Add thickness by attaching boards to the visible edges of the flats as shown here.

Simplify, Simplify

Few of us ever have all the money, space, and expertise to design and build the scenery we'd like. Consider a few of the problems confronting the designer of scenery for an evening of three one-act plays:

Quantity: Most theatres have a supply of stock scenery, flats and platforms and furniture that can be used and reused. But very few theatres have enough stock scenery to assemble three — or even two — complicated sets at the same time. And few theatres have a budget large enough to buy the materials needed to build that much new scenery.

Shifting Time: Settings that require walls made of flats *must* be attached to the floor for stability, especially if there are doors with shutters. The bracing needed is not complicated, but setting up and taking down such a set usually require more time than is available in a brief intermission between plays.

Shifting Storage: Every item of scenery that comes off the stage has to be put somewhere, and it can't be in a place that blocks the scenery you need for the next play, or the one after that.

Construction Space and Expertise: Most school theatres lack a sufficient quantity of space, tools, and/or people with the necessary knowledge and skill to permit such extensive construction projects, even if the materials for the scenery are available.

What's a poor designer to do? Simplify!

Perhaps there's a way to reduce that complete interior to just a corner of a room where a couple of flats, hinged together, will provide a background without requiring extensive bracing.

Maybe that door doesn't have to be visible to the audience, and the entrance/exit can be established as "down the hall" to the just-out-of-sight (and therefore nonexistent!) door.

The table from one play can be used in another play with the addition of a tablecloth. That armchair or sofa can be used twice or three times with different throw pillows or covers. That two-fold section of wall can be used in another play if the color is fairly neutral — and you can hang different pictures on it for each different play.

Unless a character has to actually enter or exit through the window, perhaps it could be placed in the invisible downstage "fourth wall" of the set, allowing the actors to create the illusion of a window as they face the audience.

Remember that the audience will believe anything reasonable you ask them to believe about your setting — as long as your design and the actors' performance support that belief. If the audience hears a doorbell or a knock and one of the characters says, "Oooh! He's here!" and runs off through an upstage arch (with masking) or around the corner of a flat, the audience will be happy to believe that there really is a front door over there somewhere!

Painting Scenery

Designing and building scenery is only part of the process. Before the audience sees the set, it needs to be painted. And before the painting can start, the set must be prepared and the paint selected and/or mixed. Let's take a look at the materials we'll need.

Paint

Paint, any kind of paint, is made up of three parts: *Pigment, Medium,* and *Binder.* The pigment is what gives the paint its color. These particles of color float in a medium such as water or oil. Most paints used for scenery are water-based paints. When the paint is applied, the medium dries and the binder holds the pigment to the surface.

Latex paint, popular for home use, has a latex binder. That's why water will wash it out of brushes and clothes before the paint dries but not after. Latex paint is useful for scene painting because of its easy availability and its ability to stand up to rugged use. It is waterproof when dry, so a flat can be painted over several times. Eventually, though, the layers of paint become so thick that the paint cracks and the flat must be re-covered.

Scene paint or dry pigment is the old standby for stage work. Its advantages are many. Since the pigment is purchased dry, you don't pay shipping and storage for all that water. You also don't have to store all that water in your shop. Scene paint is available in an extremely wide variety of colors and mixing the exact shade you want is easy. On the other hand, you must provide a binder when you mix scene paint. Traditionally, the binder is cooked gelatin glue, but polyvinyl glues (like Elmer's) are more convenient to use although considerably more expensive. Scene paint is not waterproof when dry; as a matter of fact, it must be washed off of flats before they can be repainted for the next show.

Poster paint is sometimes used in an emergency or for small jobs. The colors are not pure, but all you need to add is water since the binder is included.

Shellac and *Varnish* are used occasionally to give a shine to a painted

161

surface. These are now available in water-based formulations so that you don't need paint thinner or other solvents for clean-up.

Spray paint is sometimes used for small jobs or special effects. These paints, usually enamel, are most useful for painting small props that need a shiny surface. They are oil-based and paint thinner is required to remove over-spray. There is also cause for concern with the health effects of the vapors of spray paints, as well as their possible use for vandalism.

Glue and Size-Water

Flake glue or carpenter's glue must be cooked in a gluepot — sort of an electric double-boiler — before use in painting. Fill the inner container about two-thirds full with dry glue, then cover the glue with water. Plug in or turn on the glue pot, stir occasionally, and by the next morning (or several hours later) you'll have glue. This is *extremely* sticky stuff and can be used as is for regluing loose furniture joints.

Making size-water is easier if there are two people working. The idea is to mix one part of the cooked glue with about eight parts of water. Since the glue is hot and tends to harden as it cools, warm or hot water is helpful but not necessary. Put one-third to one-half the water in an empty pail or garbage can — something with a fairly tight lid. Stir vigorously as the glue is slowly poured into the water. Keep stirring as the remainder of the water is added. A small amount of phenol solution or oil of wintergreen added to the mixture will prolong its useful life (since this is an animal product, it will spoil and stink).

The size-water can be used as is for gluing down the edges of muslin on newly covered flats. To use this glue for sizing flats, mix two parts sizing with one part water. To use it for scene paint, dilute two parts sizing to one part water (for walls) or less (for benches, props — things the actors will handle or touch). Too little glue in the mixture will yield paint that rubs off; too much will cause the paint to crack and flake and possibly chip off.

White polyvinyl glue or yellow carpenter's polyvinyl glue can be substituted for animal glue. Small amounts of sizing are easy to mix, and there is no chance of spoilage. Gallon bottles are the best buy for this expensive alternate.

Dutchman

Scenery is assembled from separate pieces. A section of several flats, joined side to side, forms a flat wall. Thickness pieces are attached at every opening. Platforms have tops and sides and sometimes legs — and the legs are often hidden by a facing that keeps the audience from seeing under the platform. The carpentry used for scenery is much less finished than that used in "real" construction. How do you make those three flats look like one solid wall?

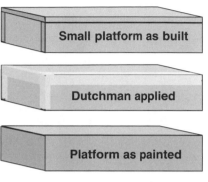

Small platform as built

Dutchman applied

Platform as painted

The answer, in a word, is *dutchman*. **Dutchman** is a strip of muslin — the same fabric used to cover the flats — that is glued over any joint you don't want the audience to see. Remember that all the edges of the muslin strip must be torn, not cut. Best results will be obtained by using a muslin strip long enough to cover the entire joint, but shorter strips can be used with the lower strip overlapping the upper one.

Dutchman should be applied to outside corners of the set, but since people expect to see a "line" at an inside corner, no dutchman is necessary. Edges of platforms, steps, door frames and other such joints should also be covered.

Remember that the object of all this gluing is to hide the joints. That's why the muslin is torn, not cut. And that's why it's important to smooth down all the edges, leaving no wrinkles or little turned-under edges. Use your fingers to smooth things if you need to — the glue will rinse off.

Mixing Paint Colors

Whether you use dry scene paint or latex paint or some other paint system, you'll need to mix the colors you want. And mixing dry pigment with size-water needs a little explaining, too.

Latex paint dries lighter than it looks as a

> ## WHAT'S WHITING?
>
> Dry pigment and size water make paint, but the paint will be *transparent* — after it dries you will be able to see through it to whatever is below. Whiting is the cheap white pigment mixed in to make the paint *opaque.* Don't confuse whiting with the more expensive white pigment used to make white paint!

liquid in the can. The only sure way to predict the outcome of mixing two or more shades of latex paint is to apply a little of the mixture to a piece of scrap lumber, for example, and see what it looks like when it dries.

Scene paint dries lighter, too. But it dries to the same shade it was before you added the size-water. Mixing colors is easier with scene paint because you can simply mix small quantities of the dry pigments. Record the proportions of your mixture (one tablespoon French yellow ochre, two spoons whiting, one-half spoon of Milori yellow light, for example), then you can mix larger quantities (one cup French yellow ochre, two cups whiting, etc.)

When the pigment is mixed in a bucket, it's time to turn it into paint by adding the size-water. This is good exercise for your arms, because you must add only a small amount of liquid at a time to the dry pigment, stirring vigorously until all of the pigment is wet — about the consistency of cake batter. If too much liquid is added too

> ## BIGGER BRUSHES BETTER
>
> **Use the biggest brush you can find for base coats. A six-inch wide brush won't fit into a gallon can of latex paint, but the time and energy saved by the big brush makes it well worth pouring the paint into a bucket. Wider brushes are almost always better — if you need to paint a piece of trim, use the brush sideways (like a make-up brush used for wrinkles)!**

soon, small clumps of pigment become coated or encapsulated with water and resist breaking up. Pigment does not dissolve in the water as cocoa mix does; it stays in suspension. If your paint is lumpy, you'll have to stick your hand in and squeeze the lumps out. Once all the pigment is wet, stir as you add more size-water to bring the mixture to painting consistency (rather like cream).

The Base Coat

The assembled set pieces, dutchman in place, are ready for painting. The first paint applied is the base coat. If you're painting an entire set, the paint should be divided into several buckets. *Stir scene paint frequently to keep the pigment from settling to the bottom.* Use the paint brush to give the paint a stir every time you dip it into the bucket.

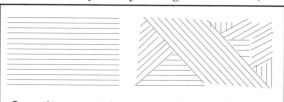

Smooth, even strokes are good for painting trim at home, but bad for painting scenery.

No matter which kind of paint you're using, be sure you paint "in all directions." Make a conscious effort not to leave visible brush strokes all going in the same direction. Why? Because brush strokes are really places where the paint is slightly thicker and slightly thinner, and the thick places will cast (small) shadows when stage lights shine on them.

One coat is all you'll need, providing you don't leave any *holidays,* small unpainted places. How long the paint takes to dry depends on the humidity in your part of the world, but be sure you allow drying time when you schedule your painting sessions. As soon as the base coat is dry you're ready for the texture coats.

Texturing

Texture coats are the secret to good-looking scenery. A good base coat, with the light-and-shadow pattern broken up by crisscross brush strokes, will most often still reveal the underlying patches and strips of dutchman

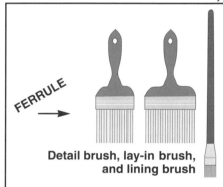

Detail brush, lay-in brush, and lining brush

because of the slight shadows cast by the straight lines of the torn edges. Texturing is like camouflage. It fools the eye of the viewer, in the same way that the highlights and shadows of stage makeup fool them.

Texturing is the application of an overall nonpattern to the entire surface. By using two different texture coats, one lighter and cooler and one darker and warmer than the base coat, you will supply artificial highlights and shadows that mask those caused by irregularities in the set. There are many different texturing techniques, but here are three of the most popular.

Spattering is best accomplished with a large brush and paint that has been thinned to the consistency of milk. Dip the brush into the paint, then remove most of the paint against the edge of the bucket. You may even want to provide some newspaper on the floor to shake out even more paint from the brush. Hold the brush by the handle and strike the ferrule (the metal band that holds the bristles to the handle) sharply against the base of your other hand's thumb. This will cause the bristles to snap forward, releasing a spray of paint. With a little practice you will be able to control the brush so that an even spray is applied, leaving a pattern of dots over the entire surface. Don't try to spatter with only one hand, slinging the brush

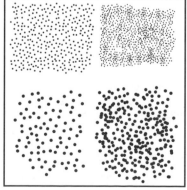

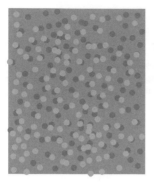
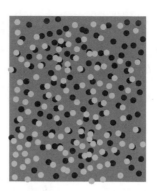

towards the flat. You will leave a discernible streak. Spattering can be done with varying sizes of dots (depending on how much paint you leave in the brush) and varying densities (depending on how many times you strike your hand with the brush in the same spot). Smaller dots make the spatter more subtle, as does keeping the spatter colors fairly close to the base color. Spattering works on the eye sort of like the little dots that make up the colors in the Sunday comics. From a distance, you don't see the dots, only the color.

Rag rolling provides a rougher-looking texture, again depending on the amount of contrast between the colors. It can be used to simulate heavy plaster or stone. Roll a burlap or muslin rag into a loose roll, then dip it into the thinned paint. Yes, you have to put your hands into the paint! Wring out the excess, then lay the rag on the set and roll it gently a few inches, leaving a random print where the rag actually touches the set. Pick up the rag and change the direction of the next roll.

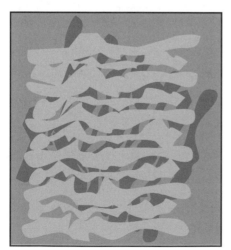

CHANGE PARTNERS AND DANCE!

When more than one person is texturing a set (or painting a drop), it's important to shift people from one area to another, exchanging places frequently. Each person will have his or her own style of applying the paint, and you need to keep the styles mixed — like brush strokes — so the set won't look like different sections were painted by different people (Even though it was! Tricky, ain't we?).

Schlepitska, or feather-dusting, is done with one of those old-fashioned dusters made from stiff turkey feathers. Gather the feathers into a tighter bundle with your hand, so they'll fit into the bucket. Wet the feathers with paint, then wring out the excess. Hold the duster by the handle and press the end of the feathers against the set. Pull the duster away, rotate it slightly, then "print" again. This method is very quick and painless — if you can find a turkey-feather duster!

Texturing isn't always random, it can also involve patterns. Applying painted lines will hide the shadow lines you don't want the audience to see. Bricks, wood paneling, wallpaper, and others can be imitated with paint. Lining is often done in addition to other texturing techniques. Use a lining brush (if you have one) and a straight-edge — being careful to hold the edge slightly off the flat so the paint won't flow under it and ruin your straight line.

The Care and Feeding of Brushes, Buckets, and Other Things Your Mother Isn't Here to Take Care Of

There are inexpensive paint brushes and there are good paint brushes. A six-inch lay-in brush with thick and springy bristles holds a lot of paint, applies paint quickly, and works well for spattering. It can cost more than forty dollars. It can last, *with proper care*, over ten years.

Local hardware stores probably don't even stock six-inch brushes. A four-inch brush can be purchased for less than five dollars. It will be thinner, hold less paint, and require more energy and time in painting. With care it can last through three or four shows.

No theatre I know of has enough money to buy good brushes every year. *Take care of your tools!*

Avoid getting paint or size-water on and under the ferrule.

Never leave a brush sitting in a bucket of paint or glue overnight.

Rinse brushes *thoroughly*. Rinse them until the water runs

clear, then rinse them again. Even a small amount of paint left in the brush when it's hung up to dry will collect in the bristles and harden. And if it's latex paint, you might just as well throw the brush away.

Hang brushes bristle down to dry.

Cover buckets containing paint you'll need tomorrow.

Clean all other buckets, leaving them upside down to dry.

Keep the paint area — including the sink — clean. Wipe up spills immediately.

Exercises:

1. Draw an accurate ¼-inch = 1 foot scale groundplan of the stage at your school's theatre.

2. Read a one-act play and develop a groundplan for your stage. Assume the play will be the only one produced and will have a large budget. *Or* assume the play will be presented as part of a double bill, with a small or nonexistent budget.

3. Prepare a report for the class about a famous theatrical designer, including pictures of his/her designs.

4. Demonstrate at least five texturing techniques by painting them on different sections of a flat.

CHAPTER SIXTEEN

FAMILY ALBUM, PART IV:
ROMANTICISM TO REALISM

From Romanticism to Realism

This section of our family album presents only a few carefully selected "snapshots," chosen largely from the English-speaking theatre. Much has been left out. There are two reasons for these omissions: theatre activity had become much more widely spread with the expansion of the United States, and — since we are talking about relatively recent times — we have access to better and more complete records of all that activity. A complete presentation of all that we know of the theatre during this period would fill volumes, and our aim is to provide — pardon the mixed metaphor — an appetizer rather than the complete seven course meal.

From "really old" to "recognizably modern" might be as good a title for this chapter, because until the late part of the nineteenth century, plays had a distinctly old-fashioned feel. By the first years of the twentieth century, theatre had become something that we will recognize as modern — much as the earliest automobiles seem fairly modern compared to earlier methods of transportation such as the chariot or the horse and buggy.

By the beginning of the nineteenth century, theatre practice already had seen many changes since the Elizabethan era. Indoor performances were the rule rather than the exception. Wing and shutter scenery and scenic spectacle were the rule. Women had returned to the stage after the English Restoration in 1660. By the beginning of the twentieth century, theatre practice had changed even more. Let's take a brief look at some of the most important developments in staging, acting and playwriting.

Staging

When theatres moved indoors in the late seventeenth and early eighteenth centuries, the scenic artist came into his own. Certainly the most prevalent form of scenery, especially in theatres with no fly space, was called *wing and shutter* because of the use of several pairs of grouped wing units on each side of the stage and a larger but similar set up center. Some of these arrangements became quite elaborate, with under-the-stage linkages and operating systems, so that scenery could be shifted without displaying any stagehands.

The downstage flat of each set was painted with the scenery for the first scene of the play. For scene two, the first set of wings (and shutters) was slid to an off-stage position to reveal the second set of wings, painted with the appropriate scenery. Additional scenes required additional sets of wings and shutters.

Theatres with fly space often used drops — large unframed pieces of fabric — for backgrounds. Scenery using these drops could be changed rapidly by lowering one drop while raising another. This technique

Groundplan of typical wing and shutter scenery, with the first or downstage wings (and shutters) shown in their off-stage positions for scene two.

remained popular in the American musical theatre well past the middle of the twentieth century.

Theatres without fly spaces, or touring companies who could not depend on finding a fully equipped theatre in every town, often used a *roll drop*. The roll drop could be painted with scenery, too, but instead of being flown up into the scene house, it rolled up around a cylinder attached to the bottom of the drop. To this day, a roll drop is often used in melodramas, those plays where the audience is supposed to cheer the hero and hiss the villain.

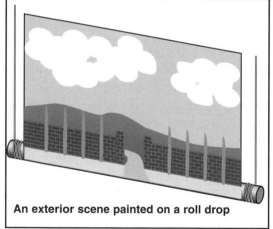

An exterior scene painted on a roll drop

While wing and shutter scenery allowed for easy scene changes, beautiful stage pictures, and many entrances/exits (between the wings) for the cast, the effect was not particularly realistic. The desire for more realism in the theatre led, during the nineteenth century, to the development of the standard *box set*. The box set was supposed to look like a room with one side (the "fourth wall") missing, so that the audience was allowed to "spy" on the actions of the characters while the characters went about their business as if the audience were not there at all. Box sets, sometimes including a ceiling, were much more realistic, and could be painted and decorated to look like a hovel or a palace or any place in between.

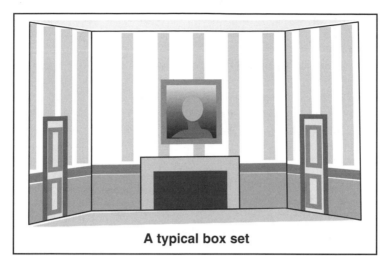

A typical box set

The Industrial Revolution reached the theatre in areas other than lighting, too. Stage machinery and equipment became increasingly common and more and more complicated. By 1880, Steele MacKaye had opened the Madison Square Theatre in New York, featuring an "elevator stage" with two "floors," capable of replacing one entire realistic set with another in only forty seconds.

The nineteenth century also saw the development of gas lights to replace candles and oil lamps for stage lighting. Variable intensity lighting became possible when a large gas-valve manifold allowed control of the gas flow to separate lights. The lime light shed its whiter, brighter light on the stage a little later and, thanks to the efforts of Thomas Edison, the electric lamp came into use in theatres before the end of the century.

Acting (and Directing)

The nineteenth century was a great time for actors. The American stage was filled with actors and actresses whose passionate performances electrified audiences. The passions of these actors, and those of their supporters, at least once created violence outside the theatre.

The Astor Place Opera House Riot in New York, May 10, 1849, came during a time of general distrust and dislike of all

JOSEPH JEFFERSON AS RIP VAN WINKLE

Jefferson, the son and grandson of actors and designers, first appeared as Rip Van Winkle in 1850. While he did play other parts, his portrayal of the title character of Washington Irving's story so captivated American audiences that he continued to play the part — in constantly revised versions of the show — for many years. He performed the part thousands of times until he finally retired in 1904.

things British or European. Supporters of American actor Edwin Forrest disrupted a performance by English actor William Macready as Macbeth. The cheers of supporters and the boos of "critics" inside the theatre were magnified by the unruly mob that gathered outside. Police in the theatre tried to arrest the disruptors, and the crowd outside was eventually quieted by troops — both mounted and infantry—who, their other efforts having failed, fired into the crowd. By the time the evening was over, twenty-two people had been killed.

The Star System

Early nineteenth-century acting had a remarkable tendency to the flamboyant and theatrical. A performance was often judged excellent because of its "theatrical effect" even though the critic might note a lack of realism in the performance. To give the actors their due, we should remember that theatres were often quite large (and without electronic amplification!), requiring loud voices and large gestures, and that audiences expected the actor to display his or her virtuosity and technical skills even at the expense of reality.

The star system that developed in the nineteenth century brought the actor to the fore. Playwrights and theatre managers and designers all played second fiddle to the actor. As is most often the case, this state of affairs had both good and bad consequences.

On the good side, the star system brought famous performers to almost every city, town and hamlet. Edwin

> ### BREECHES PARTS
> The nineteenth century saw many male roles played by women. Charlotte Cushman, for example, played Romeo and Hamlet; Fanny Vining, Melinda Jones, and Mrs. Shaw also played Romeo; Sarah Bernhardt played Hamlet. This gave actresses a chance to expand beyond the limited female roles in the classics — and drew audiences to the theatre to see again plays that were already so familiar as to be not worth the price of admission.

Forrest, Charles and Fanny Kemble, Edmund Kean, the Booths (yes, the American theatrical family that included John Wilkes Booth of Ford's

No star ever seemed bright enough to illuminate the rest of the cast

Theatre/Abraham Lincoln fame), Joseph Jefferson, William Gillette, Sarah Bernhardt, Eleanora Duse... all these and more made names for themselves on the nineteenth-century American stage.

The plays they brought to the growing American nation

provided not only entertainment, but also a connection to the cultural life of the world. Their appearances in both classics and new plays were eagerly awaited. The theatre was, after all, a good place for those interested in culture and (especially) society to be seen.

On the other hand, the star system eventually had a terrible effect on the level of performance and staging. Imagine what it would be like to be an actor in a repertory company, scheduled to present a "star" vehicle. Sometimes the star would arrive only a day before the performance, with manuscript copies of the script for you to learn by the next evening! Rehearsal time was almost nonexistent, and even when the play was a familiar classic such as *Romeo and Juliet*, the "local" cast would have no way to explore the nuances of the script with the leading actor or actress, leading to a stilted performance. As a matter of fact, audiences often found the star occupying center stage alone, while the supporting cast hovered at the edges of the stage, muttering and mumbling the unfamiliar dialog.

> ## THE DIVINE SARAH BERNHARDT
>
> This French actress toured the United States several times in her long career, beginning in 1880. Her reputation as a wonderful actress was enhanced by her personal eccentricities. She injured her knee on-stage in the early twentieth century, and ten years later that leg was finally amputated because of gangrene, but Sarah Bernhardt continued to tour for several years, playing roles that could be performed while seated. *The show must go on!*

The change to realism in acting — in America and around the world — is today best known through the work of Konstantin Stanislavsky who, with Vladimir Nemirovich-Danchenko opened the Moscow Art Theatre in 1898. Stanislavsky and his ensemble of actors developed a system of acting in which purely theatrical effects were abandoned in favor of identifying with the character using the actor's own psychological and physical responses, "living" the part. His system proved so successful that it has influenced actors for almost a hundred years so far.

The Rise of the Director

The star system declined when audiences began to demand greater realism on the stage. This demand came about at the same time as the development of the director as the controlling element in theatrical production. In Europe, the Duke of Saxe-Meiningen and others were experimenting with unified productions: historically accurate costumes, scenery designed and built to fit a particular production, *all* actors — leading roles, supporting roles, even minor roles and walk-ons — trained and then restrained from the excesses of overblown romantic acting.

In the United States, Steele MacKaye and David Belasco (among others) made names for themselves by producing and directing plays with more realism in scenery, reproducing on-stage the more spectacular effects of nature. A stage version of Lew Wallace's novel, *Ben Hur*, was presented by another producer in prelude, six acts, and fourteen scenes. The movement of all those "acres of scenery," the accurate costuming, and the rehearsed performances of even the Roman slaves combined to create an unforgettable — if very expensive — stage spectacle.

The director soon took over each production, making all decisions to create a performance in which each element contributed to a single artistic aim. The stage actor has never regained the almost unlimited power that he or she had in the early and middle nineteenth century. Today's actors may move us to tears and laughter, they may be the objects of adoration and fan clubs, but they do not control the entire production, bending every element to enhance their own — and only their own — reputation.

Plays and Playwrights

American playwriting in the nineteenth century left few enduring marks in our family album. Stage adaptations of Harriet Beecher Stowe's *Uncle Tom's Cabin* were popular. Anna Cora Mowatt's comedy, *Fashion,* is still remembered but rarely (if ever) produced any longer. Most of the excitement in playwriting came around the turn of the century, and most of it came from across the Atlantic Ocean.

Scandinavia

Henrik Ibsen was a Norwegian dramatist who became known as the Father of Modern Drama. He broke away from the popular formula of the "well-made play." His playwriting career included *Peer Gynt,* written in 1867, a nationalistic, romantic (and poetic) play based on a Norwegian legend, probably better known today because of the incidental music composed for it by Ibsen's compatriot Edvard Grieg. When his *A Doll's House* opened in 1879, its realistic and unsentimental treatment of Nora, who recognizes her powerlessness and so leaves her husband and family, was considered so scandalous and vile that many audience members walked out of the performance before the closing

THE WELL-MADE PLAY

French playwright Eugene Scribe is credited with developing this "formula for successful plays": a plot that revolves around some unknown but vital factor, a structure of rising suspense, and a climax (or obligatory scene) in which the mystery factor is revealed — usually in such a way as to save the protagonist from a dangerous situation. These plays tend toward the farcical and melodramatic, and are essentially empty of serious content or realistic characters. Has Hollywood been told that this went out of style before 1900?

curtain. His later plays, all delving into the psychology and social effects of people living in modern society, included *Ghosts* (the effects of venereal disease, written in 1881), and *Hedda Gabler,* (1890, an examination of the relationships between love, greed, and power — again featuring a strong female character). He also wrote *An Enemy of the People* and *The Wild Duck.* His plays caused an uproar whenever they were translated and performed, but his insistence on dealing with the inner truth of individuals and their relationships with each other made him distinctly modern — and immortal.

August Strindberg, the Swedish playwright, was perhaps even more introspective. His long one-act *Miss Julie,* first produced in 1888, is still much admired and often produced. It tells the story of a young woman of the upper class who seduces her father's footman — with serious consequences. One of his later plays, *The Dance of Death* (1901), deals with a tyrannical but dying husband who has kept his wife more or less enslaved, and her efforts to exact revenge.

Russia

The late stages of the Russian Empire were chronicled by Anton Chekhov. Chekhov was educated as a doctor, but his ill health forced him to live a calmer and quieter life. He was well known for his short stories, and his short plays, especially *The Boor* and *The Marriage Proposal*, are frequently performed. His first long play, *The Seagull,* was poorly received on its opening in 1896, and Chekhov determined to write no more plays. Fortunately, the play was revived to rave reviews by the fledgling Moscow Art Theatre, and Chekhov's continued efforts have given us some of the world's greatest plays. *Uncle Vanya* (1899), *The Three Sisters* (1901), and *The Cherry Orchard* (1904) are his only other full-length plays, but Chekhov's genius at revealing universal humanity through the remnants of a particular dying society is amply revealed.

> **CHEKHOV AND THE MOSCOW ART THEATRE**
>
> **Chekhov's playwriting career was "saved" by the Moscow Art Theatre production of *The Seagull*, but it was a two-way street. The theatre profited so much from its association with Chekhov that it adopted a seagull as its visual symbol or logo!**

In *The Three Sisters*, we find the three women (and their brother) living in a small provincial town. They dream — and talk — of returning to the active social scene in Moscow, and meanwhile marry, carry on extramarital affairs, and suffer separate but intense disappointments. Their dreams are never realized, but their dreams are what sustain them. Chekhov's ability to combine comedy, pathos, drama, and true psychological insight has seldom been equaled.

175

Ireland

The Abbey Theatre, opened in Dublin in 1904 for the production of plays by Irish writers and about Ireland, was an important part of what was called the Irish Renaissance. For thirty years or so, the Abbey Theatre was home to controversial playwrights and performances. William Butler Yeats, Lady Gregory, John Millington Synge, (and later Sean O'Casey) were associated with the early days of the Abbey Theatre.

One of the masterpieces of the period was 1907's *The Playboy of the Western World*, written by **John Millington Synge.** In this play, Christy Mahon, believing he has murdered his father, runs away from home. His telling of the tale to the residents of a small village results in his elevation to hero status — until his father (quite alive) arrives on the scene. The plot is simple, there are plenty of laughs, but Synge's passionate and soaring use of the English language is awesome.

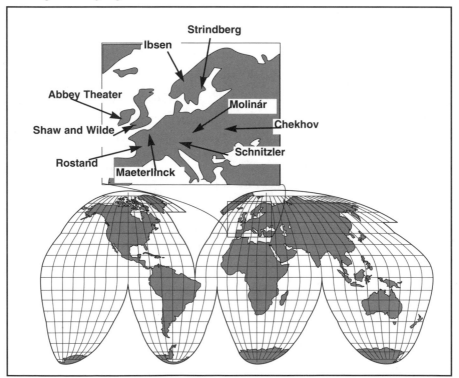

England

Oscar Wilde published only two memorable full-length plays: *Lady Windermere's Fan* (1892) and *The Importance of Being Earnest* (1895), but his clever, witty look at British manners and society have assured his plays of continued attention. In *The Importance of Being Earnest,* young Jack Worthing wishes to marry Gwendolyn Fairfax, daughter of Lady Bracknell. Lady Bracknell is opposed to the marriage because he lacks a family background — as an infant he was found in a handbag in the left-luggage area of a train station. Jack's friend Algernon Moncrieff — who wants to marry Jack's ward, Cecily Cardew — turns out to be Jack's older brother (and Jack is "really" Ernest Moncrieff) when it is discovered that Jack was forgotten in the station by an absentminded governess. Jack is delighted, because he had *invented* a brother Ernest, whose continual scrapes and difficulties gave Jack an excuse to get away from his country home to visit Gwendolyn in London. And besides, Gwendolyn has always wanted to marry a man named Ernest!

George Bernard Shaw was a writer and social critic of immense energy. He began writing plays in 1885 and continued until his death in 1950 at the age of ninety-four. *Arms and the Man* (1894) and *Cæsar and Cleopatra* (1899) are two of his best earlier plays.

Major Barbara (1905) is a superb example of his social conscience. The title character, an officer in the Salvation Army, must come to terms with her reaction to large donations of "tainted" money from a whiskey distiller and an armaments manufacturer.

Perhaps his best known play is *Pygmalion* (1913), which was adapted by Lerner and Lowe for their musical, *My Fair Lady.* Shaw examined the rigid social structure of his time, the uses and abuses of "the King's English," and the relationships between men and women. Characters such as the erudite Professor Henry Higgins, the flower-girl-turned-lady, Eliza Doolittle, and her ne'er-do-well father will remain popular for years and years to come.

Shaw's version of the story of Joan of Arc, *Saint Joan,* was produced in 1923, shortly after her canonization by the Catholic church. It shows Joan as a young woman who puts her conscience ahead of the judgment of the church. She dies because her ideas are dangerous to both the church and her feudal society. In an ironic epilogue, Joan is informed of her new status as a saint and, surprised, she offers to return to earth. In what is the usual fate of saints and geniuses — at least according to Shaw — she is again rejected.

France

Edmond Rostand is best known in the English speaking world for his romantic drama, *Cyrano de Bergerac* (1897). The play tells the story of the poet-actor-soldier with a beautiful soul and a very large nose. Cyrano loves Roxanne, but believing his nose makes him unlovable, helps his friend Christian win her hand. When Christian is killed in battle, Roxanne retires to a convent where Cyrano visits her daily, not revealing his love for her — or learning of hers for him — until the day of his death.

Belgium

Maurice Maeterlinck also wrote romantic plays. His *Pelléas et Melisande* (1892), an antirealistic examination of forbidden love, includes supernatural influences. It was reworked as an opera by Debussy in 1902. *The Bluebird* (1909), while also romantic in tone, was more hopeful in spirit.

Hungary

Ferenc Molnár wrote over thirty plays (in addition to his novels and short stories), but the one best known today is *Liliom* (1909). This story of the innocent girl and the worldly carnival barker is easily recognizable as the source of the story in the Rodgers and Hammerstein musical, *Carousel*.

Austria

Arthur Schnitzler wrote plays with what we think of as the typical Viennese wit and amoral attitude toward erotic situations. He is best remembered for his play, *La Ronde* (1896, published 1903). Schnitzler examines "love" in a series of interlocking scenes — prostitute and husband, husband and wife, wife and lover, lover and...ending again with the prostitute as in the first scene.

Exercises:

1. Build a working scale model of a roll drop. Make the drop at least a foot wide and nine inches high; double that size would be better.
2. Prepare a class presentation in which you compare and contrast the plot, theme and characters of *Pygmalion* and *My Fair Lady*.
3. Research and build a working salt-water (or soapy-water) dimmer as a model of those used early in the days of electricity in theatres.
4. Read about and write a biographical report about one of the great actors (or families of actors) of the nineteenth century.
5. Enact a scene from one of the plays from this period.

CHAPTER SEVENTEEN

PROPS, COSTUMES, AND SOUND

Producing a play involves paying great attention to details. Using the props, costumes, and sounds that are just right can make a big difference in the overall effect of the play on the audience. Unfortunately, few high school theatre programs have enough equipment and skilled technicians to create the perfect props, costumes, and sound effects — nor do they have money to buy or even rent them, either. All too often, the students assigned to these crews are left to their own devices and believe that their jobs aren't important to the efforts of the whole group.

What can be done? Once again, it's time for creativity and diligence to take the place of money! First, let's take a look at those activities and responsibilities that are common to all these crews.

Planning and Preparation

First, read the script. Second, read the script again, listing all the information from the script that is pertinent to your crew (props used or pointed out in the dialog, descriptions of costumes worn by each character in each scene, sound cues such as telephone bells, door buzzers, radios blaring, and so on. Transfer all this information to a neat and legible list, then confer with the director and/or designer to coordinate your actions, making sure that you haven't forgotten something (or have on your list something that the director has decided should be omitted).

Check the rehearsal schedule. Plan to attend as many rehearsals as possible. You must attend every rehearsal and performance from first technical rehearsal on, and most directors will require your presence earlier than that. Clear your own schedule of all possible conflicts.

Properties

Generally speaking, anything that is carried by a cast member is called a hand prop: a book, a glass, a pitcher, a camera, a suitcase, a book of matches, etc. Larger items, and/or those that are never picked up by the actors, are called set props. At this level of theatre all the smaller items that are more properly called set decorations come under the aegis of the prop crew: pictures on the walls, a blotter on the desk, vases of flowers, and so on.

There is one small area that sometimes causes disagreement. Cast members carry purses, and sometimes gloves and hats, too. Are these items props or costumes? How about eyeglasses, especially those provided for the show because of their historical or other style that suits the character rather than the actor? Each theatre group reaches its own agreement over the responsibility for items like these, but if you are on the prop crew, be sure you know how far your responsibilities extend!

There are four options for acquiring the props for a play.

1. Props may be pulled from stock. Most theatre groups have a collection of dishes and flatware, for example.

2. Props may be borrowed. Check with your teacher or director before you borrow expensive items. The school or theatre group may not be able or willing to assume financial responsibility for damage to or loss of private property.

3. Props may be built. Sash cord glued in a serpentine pattern to a plastic mug, then painted gold or silver might make a medieval chalice (but don't try to drink from it).

4. Props may be purchased. Artificial flowers, inexpensive glassware, a cast-off toaster, bargain wall decorations — a drama teacher or prop crew head needs to become familiar with local discount, second-hand, and distressed-merchandise stores.

> ### SUBSTITUTE PROPS?
>
> On your rehearsal schedule, usually just about the time the cast goes off book, you'll notice an entry that reads, "Substitute Props." On that day you must be sure that the cast has *something* to carry or use, even if it's not the real prop you're still building or searching for. A paper cup for a goblet, an old briefcase for a suitcase, a stick for a knife — these are substitutes that allow the actors to begin working with their hands, but save the more expensive, fragile, or difficult-to-find props for later in the rehearsal period.

What will be the primary method of acquisition for your show? It depends! That's a large part of the problem for prop crews: nothing seems definite; everything *depends*. It's helpful to have prop crew members who can drive or who have access to transportation (How else can you haunt the second-hand stores?), but more important are those who have imagination, organization, perseverance, and tact.

Prop crews need imagination. How can we use free or inexpensive materials to make something look like an expensive antique? Can we put covers on the pillows from Act I and use them again in Act III?

Prop crews need organization. Props not only need finding or making, they need storing, using, and returning. Borrowed props must be carefully identified and safely stored for return to their owners. Property plots must be prepared for every scene of the play, showing which props are placed where on the set, which ones are placed off stage right, which off left, and so on.

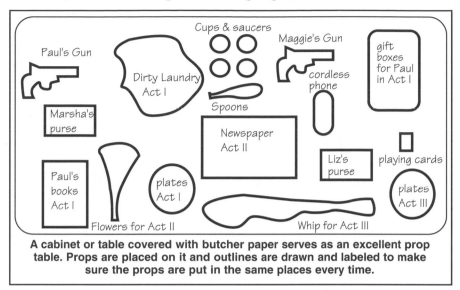

Paul's Gun

Cups & saucers

Dirty Laundry
Act I

Spoons

Maggie's Gun

cordless
phone

gift
boxes
for Paul
in Act I

Marsha's
purse

Newspaper
Act II

Paul's
books
Act I

plates
Act I

Liz's
purse

playing cards

plates
Act III

Flowers for Act II

Whip for Act III

A cabinet or table covered with butcher paper serves as an excellent prop table. Props are placed on it and outlines are drawn and labeled to make sure the props are put in the same places every time.

Prop crews need perseverance. Every prop must be taken from storage and distributed according to the plot for every rehearsal and every performance. Every prop must be returned to storage after every rehearsal and every performance. When the show closes, props owned by the theatre must be returned to long-term storage during strike; and borrowed props must be returned as soon as possible, accompanied (or followed quickly) by a written note of thanks. And there is no applause from the audience for your work. Only theatre people truly understand how difficult, time consuming, and important your work really is.

Prop crews need tact. They must confer with the director and designer. They must be able to talk to merchants, often on the telephone, in their search for props. They must arrange to borrow

THE CARE & FEEDING OF ACTORS

A prop crew should treat actors as if they are very small children who are not very bright. I can say this because I've been both an actor and a prop crew member. It's not enough to arrange the props on the prop table. A crew member must be there to hand the prop to the actor who is on his or her way to make an entrance, with perhaps a whispered, "Break a leg!" for encouragement. And when the actor comes off-stage, the crew must be there to say, "Good scene!" and take the prop again, otherwise the well-meaning actor may carry it away to the dressing room or elsewhere and it will never be seen again.

certain props, assuring their owners of their safe return. And they must deal with actors during rehearsals and performances.

Costumes

Costume crews are much like prop crews in that there is frequently neither enough money nor enough expertise to build new costumes for every show. Costumes are often pulled from stock, borrowed from the closets and drawers of the cast (and others), sometimes rented, and sometimes sewn by students or their parents. In other words, there is very little opportunity for the costume designer to actually *design* clothes for a show as is done in the professional theatre.

Nevertheless, it is helpful for the costume crew to be familiar with the historical period of the play and to know the script. While searching for clothes to put on your actors, your knowledge of the appropriate line and silhouette will help you decide between bell-bottoms or pegged trousers, for example. Your knowledge of the script and characters will help you select colors and styles appropriate for the characters and for the audience: antagonists might wear colors that clash with each other, for example.

Organizing and taking care of the costumes for the show is an important job. It requires the same perseverance and tact as working on the prop crew.

A FEW WORDS ABOUT HISTORICAL ACCURACY

Historical accuracy is wonderful — up to a point. Trying to provide it can drive you crazy, especially when there is no budget for costumes. It helps if you learn the concept of "What they don't notice won't hurt us." Take shoes, for example. If you can't provide the patent leather opera pumps called for in the stage directions for the leading man, have him wear black oxfords, well polished and shined. Unless the shoes are the focus of the scene, the audience will most likely never notice what he has on his feet — as they certainly would notice if he wore tennis shoes!

Costumes selected for a particular cast member should be hung on a rack behind a cardboard divider with the actor's or character's name on it.

You must see to it that costumes are maintained in good condition. Actors should be checked before each entrance to be sure their costumes are correctly worn and look clean — if they're supposed to be clean. You'll need a clothes brush of some sort. A needle and thread (for sewing on buttons or tacking a hem) should be handy, as well as a supply of straight pins and safety pins.

During a long run, or if other conditions demand it, the costumes will need to be washed and ironed between performances. In the high school theatre, this usually means taking the shirts (or whatever) home with you and remembering to bring them back the next day — or sending them home with the cast and making sure they bring them back.

Sound Effects

Technology has left school theatre in the lurch in the area of sound effects. Only a few years ago a sound crew could prepare an excellent "soundtrack" for a play by copying selected portions of record albums onto quarter-inch tape on an open reel (or reel-to-reel) tape recorder, then splicing the tape into the right order using leader (nonmagnetic) tape to separate the final selections. Nowadays, open reel tape recorders are unavailable except in studio quality (and studio price!) equipment, and it's getting harder and harder to maintain our old turntables. Even finding quarter-inch splicing tape and equipment can be difficult.

Music to be played before the show, at intermission, or after the show can perhaps be played directly from a CD, since there are usually no specific cues or timings involved. Other sounds, those that are part of the action of the play, present a different problem. Because they must be played exactly on cue (when the actor turns on the stereo, for example, or when the dialog needs the cry of a wolf to make sense), playing them from a CD — or even a record album — is scarcely appropriate.

Cassette tapes are available in a wide variety of lengths, including endless loops that come in handy for continuing effects like wind blowing around the eaves of the old house. By recording the effect exactly at the beginning of the cassette (allowing for the nonmagnetic leader), it is possible to build a collection of cassettes to be played one after another during the performance. Sound cues that can be a little "looser," an off-stage marching band that approaches from a distance, perhaps, might be recorded later on a cassette, following a timed silence (so the crew will know when to stop the tape after the earlier sound is over but before the later sound begins to play). In any event, you can see that being organized, labeling everything, and writing things down are extremely important.

Recorded Vs. Live

Some sound effects (music as well as exotic bird calls or trains passing, for example) are best recorded and played back through your theatre sound system. Some sound effects (telephones and doorbells ringing, for example) are best done live, because it is nearly impossible for a tape-recorded telephone bell to stop ringing the instant the actor picks up the receiver.

Other effects can be done live, too. An effective gunshot can be achieved by stepping on one end of a board with the front part of your foot, then holding up the other end of a board with your fingertips. When you let go with your fingers, the weight of your foot and body will cause the board to slap against the floor with a very loud report. It's not too difficult to build a wooden "wind" machine — it sounds like wind but doesn't stir the air. Other such devices — many from the days of radio drama — can be found in specialized technical-theatre textbooks. Live sound effects are traditionally assigned to the prop crew, although each theatre develops its own policies.

An old radio should sound like an old radio, not a boom box.

Be careful when you mix sources, some live and some recorded. An audience will usually accept either, but the difference in sound (the ambience) will often startle listeners if you change back and forth.

RECORDING YOUR OWN EFFECTS

If you decide to go "on location" with a good quality tape recorder, be prepared to spend time searching for the right sound. It's strange but true that a recording of actual traffic noises may sound to the audience like surf at the beach! One sound technician needed a "splash" as something was supposedly dropped into the pond or lake. He discovered that the way to make a sound the audience would hear as the splash of an object going into the water was to record the sound of an object being pulled out of the water. Always listen, with your eyes closed, to hear what they'll hear.

Affordable Technology

A synthesizer is an electronic device that is currently available in low-cost models. If your school has one or you can borrow one, a synthesizer can be used to create a wide variety of sounds for recording on tape or live play during the show. Of course, the bigger and more expensive synthesizers provide more useful options. Sigh.

Exercises:

1. Read a one-act or full-length play and prepare a property plot.

2. Read a one-act or full-length play and prepare a costume plot.

3. Read a one-act or full-length play and prepare a sound plot and cue sheets.

4. Demonstrate the use of "old-fashioned" live sound-effect machines by researching and building a wind machine, or a rain machine, or a machine to simulate marching feet, etc.

CHAPTER EIGHTEEN
GETTING TO WORK

Making a Living in the Theatre

The theatre is a seductive lover. Nothing else quite equals the feeling of power, the joy of life lived to its fullest, as playing a part in a live play. A few fortunate people even attain star status, especially in the movies and on television, earning not only a great deal of money but the adulation of millions of fans. But there is a price.

Stories abound of the terrible temptations and ruined lives of child and adult actors. It is not our purpose here to recount them. Let's just take a look at the reality of the working actor.

Where the Action Is

First, you'll need to move to either New York (for stage work) or Los Angeles (for movie and television work). Even though the regional theatres in this country have grown bigger and stronger, New York and L.A. are where it's at.

Find a cheap place to live. And I mean cheap. Housing in either city isn't easy to find, and something you can afford may require a severe change in what you are willing to accept in terms of cleanliness and tastefulness.

Get an answering service or an answering machine. You don't want to miss any calls from agents, producers, directors — or anybody else.

Get a night job. Something that will pay the rent and maybe buy a little food and pay for your pictures and your classes. Something that allows you to spend your days knocking on doors, first seeking representation by an established agent, and then auditions for parts.

Enroll in acting classes. No matter how good you are, or how many acting classes you've taken before, or how many parts you played in school, classes are a must to maintain or improve your skills. And they do cost money.

Knock on doors. First, you need an agent, someone to represent you, to send you out for auditions, to be the middleman between you and the producers, directors, and casting offices of the world. Even after you find an agent, you'll still need to knock on doors, because it's your job to get you hired, not your agent's.

Thin Skin, Thick Skin

A professional actor needs to be possessed of contradictory qualities. On the one hand, you must appear on stage or screen as practically transparent, with every nerve ending exposed, open to every psychological breeze from those around you or from your own inner self. On the other hand, you must have a thick skin in order to withstand the constant rejection of your efforts and yourself, not letting the rejection cast you deep into the slough of despondency and despair.

Door-to-Door Sales

A door-to-door vacuum cleaner salesman leads a tough life. Most of the people he talks to every day don't want to buy what he has for sale, and many of them are downright hostile. But that's a better life than an aspiring actor's! You see, the vacuum cleaner salesman can always say, "No wonder people don't want to buy this stupid vacuum cleaner! It's a piece of...!" But the aspiring actor *is* the vacuum cleaner, and constant rejection often leads to depression and total loss of self-esteem.

Unions, Agents and Catch-22

One of your goals as an aspiring actor will be to get your union card. The primary unions for performers are these:

Screen Actors Guild (SAG): Covers all work done on film, even if it's to be shown on television.

American Federation of Television and Radio Artists (AFTRA): Covers all work done on videotape.

American Guild of Variety Artists (AGVA): Covers live work in clubs, etc.

Actors Equity: Covers work on the legitimate stage (live theatre).

Getting a union card is like getting an agent. You have to have experience. And you can't get experience without an agent and/or a union card. Well, they *do* have those open auditions, known as cattle calls (Does that tell you something about the atmosphere?), where anybody and his or her cousin can show his or her "stuff." But they only have those when they're really desperate. (Still, that's the way many actors get their "big" break.)

Of course, union membership and good representation are no guarantee of anything. These are the strangest labor unions in the world, where on any given

---

Out-of-State Cards

The unions have branches in major cities around the country. You might be able to qualify for membership before you move to New York or L.A., if you live in a place where professional work is done. There is often less competition for small roles, and the initiation fee might even be smaller!

So, you wanna be an
ACTOR?

Here's the best advice you'll ever get:

If you can think of anything else in the whole wide world — *anything* else — that you might like to do with your life,

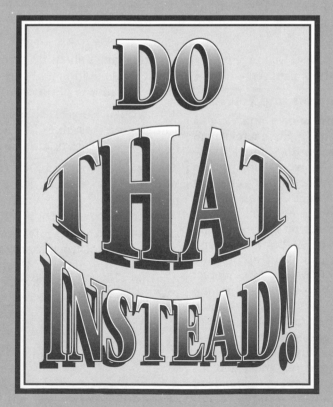

day upwards of ninety percent of the members are out of work, and where ninety-five percent of the money is earned annually by only five percent of the members.

What's It All Mean?

It means you should only become an actor for love, not for money. It means you should try to find something else to do with your life. If you truly love the theatre, consider working in some related area where employment is steadier and less dependent on having the right "look" on a particular day.

Good with words? Be a playwright. Or a screen writer. Or a publicist. Or a program-notes author.

Good in math and science? Be a theatre engineer, designing and building new theatres and new theatrical equipment.

Like to work with your hands? Be a stagehand. Or a scene painter. Or a seamstress or tailor for a costume company.

Got a good head for business? Work in the "front of the house." Sell tickets. Manage the concession stand. Arrange for promotions and product tie-ins.

Are you so well-organized your friends laugh about it? Become a professional stage manager — a good one (with a reputation for being good) can find work almost all the time.

Agents and You

Television shows and movies and even TV commercials go on location to almost every part of the world, so there is some likelihood that you'll run into somebody somewhere who wants to be your agent. An agent works on commission, a percentage of the money you earn. **If you meet an "agent" who wants *money from you up front*, run, don't walk, to the nearest exit.** It is, however, legitimate for an agent to require you to provide professional-quality photos (not cheap), and résumés, and it's fair for an agent to recommend that you take (and pay for) classes.

Are you artistic? Become a designer of scenery or costumes or advertising materials for plays or movies.

Do you have none of these talents, but still love the theatre? Then there are plenty of other jobs, even in such areas as food service (movie crews have caterers and craft service people), driving a car or truck (transporting cast and crew from hotel to location), electricians, greensman, wrangler, animal handler, editor, sound recordist, cinematographer, makeup artist, boom operator...just check the credits at the end of a major motion picture. These guys even have a staff nurse and accountants galore!

There are plenty of opportunities for you to exercise your love for theatre without becoming an actor. Educational theatre is one possibility. (Hey! There are worse jobs than being a high school drama teacher!) And most cities and towns have some kind of community theatre, where local folks with other "day jobs" get together to produce plays "just for the pure joy and love of it."

Exercises:

1. Write to one of the performers' unions, or to the International Alliance of Theatrical and Stage Employees (the union for stagehands and movie projectionists) to find out membership requirements. Present your findings to the class.

2. Find out how one becomes a member of the Directors Guild, or the Writers Guild, or any of the other professional organizations in theatre and movies. Report to the class.

APPENDIX A
THOUGHTS ON ACTING

Technique, Instinct, and "The Method"

Acting is one of the most complex behaviors of human beings. It has been cussed and discussed, dissected and analyzed, deconstructed and reconstructed by many great teachers and actors and directors, many (if not all) of them more qualified than I. Nevertheless, I want to put down on paper a few of my own thoughts — perhaps as much to help me clarify them for myself as for any help they may give to others.

Long ago I learned that some actors are "born." They seem to have an instinct for making the right choices of intonations, movements, and gestures to bring their characters to life. Others no less competent seem to use technique consciously, applying observation, trial and error, reason and thought, to the task at hand. As I was told then, and as I have observed since, it matters less from which position an actor begins and more where he or she ends. An *instinctual* actor can seem wild and uncontrolled, just as a *technical* actor can seem mannered and artificial, but a *good* actor always seems to have made the right choices. His or her performance is always fresh, always commands the attention of the audience.

Some actors and acting teachers say that good acting is a process of wrapping the actor in ever-thicker layers of disguise: makeup, costume, movements, gestures, voice — all designed and chosen to hide from the audience the true identity of the actor. Some of the most honored actors of the twentieth century have reported their own opinions that "What I'm thinking about on-stage is of no concern to the audience. The only thing that matters is what they can see and hear. If I'm thinking about tomorrow's laundry list during the Romeo and Juliet love scene, but the audience sees and hears only a love-sick youth, then I have done my job."

Other respected and well-known actors proclaim the opposite, that good acting is a process of stripping away the actor's guards and shields to reveal the truth of the human being inside. Marlon Brando, Dustin Hoffman, and many graduates of the Actors Studio (where *The Method* is king) tell us that their inner lives — thoughts and emotions — are of primary importance, governing their actions and words, allowing them to reveal the truth of their characters as aspects of their own inner selves.

The adherents of the two sides have cast many aspersions — some funny and some not — on each other over the years, but it seems to me that

193

perhaps both "sides" are correct. We all have a tendency to see and talk about the world (or acting) in the language of those who taught us. Those who have studied acting "from the outside in," beginning with body and voice, are most apt to sneer at "method" actors as undisciplined emotional slobs. Those who have studied acting "from the inside out," (the Method or another version of Stanislavsky's system of acting) are most apt to label others as slaves to technique and empty of truth.

Perhaps both sides are correct. Or maybe they're both wrong. Maybe some parts in some plays demand a more external approach. Maybe other plays require an internal, subjective performance. Maybe the difference has more to do with what is *fashionable* than what is *right*.

In any case, the audience seems to know what is right. Some actors electrify an audience. Their performances delight and inspire us — and we simply don't care whether they use technique or instinct or careful training — because we haven't time or inclination even to ask that question while the actor works his magic on the stage.

Does that mean that *talent* is all? That training and experience don't matter? Certainly not. A highly talented but unschooled and undisciplined actor is only as good as his or her current part and current director. A less-talented but well-trained and disciplined actor can be depended on to give a competent performance almost every time — and an inspired performance when play, director, and other factors combine fortuitously.

It seems to me that acting is a two-fold process. First the actor must prepare his or her body, voice, mind, and emotions to be as strong and flexible as possible — able to accomplish any task set by playwright or director. Then the actor must cast himself free, to sail upon the "sea" of the performance as Columbus set forth from Spain: confident in his preparation and skill, and ready to sense and take advantage of every nuance of wind and water on the journey.

And if everything goes right, if the actor holds fearlessly to the power of the play's "sea," great acting will happen.

APPENDIX B
EXERCISE IN BASIC STAGE MOVEMENT

This scene for two actors may be played in many styles, comically or seriously. Because the dialog is essentially meaningless, a wide variety of characters may be selected to play the scene. It is most important that you choose definite and specific characters, preferably with opposite character traits (brash/shy, old/young, bored/excited, etc.).

(Character A is discovered UC, doing something in character. B enters in character.)

B   Good morning!

A   Oh! Where did you come from?

B   *(Gesturing)* From off-stage in the wings. I'm _____.

A   And I'm _____.

B   I know. *(Pause, as B looks at A.)*

A   What are you going to do?

B   I'm crossing you to play my big scene right center. *(After B crosses, B stops.)* When I cross, you're supposed to counter-cross.

A   *(Doing so.)* Oh, sorry.

B   No, no. Move your upstage foot first. *(B begins to recite something. A goes back and does the cross correctly, but keeps moving to chair at LC.)* Don't move while I'm speaking. The attention should be on me and you're stealing the scene.

A   But I just came over here to sit down and be out of the way.

B   Yes, but attention will go to the person who is moving. Besides, every movement should have a purpose. Stage business should reveal character. *(B begins cross to R of A.)*

A   Oh! ...You make me feel all sad and stupid — like a loser.

B   *(Completing the cross to A)* Don't sit there and mope about it.

A   You're right. I must regain control. *(Rising)* Attention will go to you if you're higher.

B   And to you if I'm turned in a three-quarters back position. I'll open up and regain the attention of the audience.

A   That's not fair, being farther downstage. Is it?

B   Not fair! You're the scene stealer...oozing all that self-pity. *(Moving away)* I want nothing more to do with you.

A   *(Crossing to B)* No, I'm not a scene stealer. Please don't say that.

B   Right now you're upstaging me...again. *(A moves down.)* That's better. I like people to share the scene with me. *(B begins to recite again, then stops.)* Why don't you recite something instead of calling attention to me by staring?

A   I'm thinking about what you said and reacting before I speak.

B   You should. I admire you for trying, but you're so_____ I want nothing more to do with you. I won't even speak to you. *(B turns away and/or moves away.)*

A   Oh, please play the scene with me.

B   No. Definitely no! You heard me the first time.

A   But if you won't play the scene with me, who will?

B   I don't know, and I don't care. And furthermore, I'm leaving. *(B exits.)*

A   Well, wait for me! *(A exits.)*

Reprinted with permission of the author, Jack Frakes

JOB DESCRIPTIONS & RESPONSIBILITIES AND COMPANY RULES

Every play-producing organization — school, college, professional or community theatre — requires the coordinated efforts of many people. This section contains crew head and stage manager job descriptions as well as company rules developed for use in a high school theatre program. They are presented here to give you an idea of the specific activities involved in each of the major areas of play production.

Stage Manager

The Stage Manager's job is to

MAKE THINGS RUN SMOOTHLY.

BEFORE AUDITIONS

1. Read the script and prepare the prompt book, with blank copies of all cue sheets, worksheets, and plots needed for the show.

AT AUDITIONS

1. Set the stage.
2. Distribute and collect scripts.
3. Distribute and collect audition information cards.
4. Maintain decorum in audition waiting areas.
5. Post call-back list.

AT REHEARSALS

1. Set the stage so that rehearsal can begin promptly.
2. Prepare and distribute cast/crew phone list.
3. Distribute rehearsal schedules and company rules.
4. Control scripts.
5. Insure promptness of cast and crews.

6. Hold book, and call cues (phone & doorbells, black-outs...)
7. Maintain cast and crew morale.
8. Coordinate and record the work of all crew heads.
9. Plan and rehearse shifts with the shifting crew.

At Tech and Dress Rehearsals

1. Call each act and scene in dressing rooms and green room.
2. Give cues to lights, sound, shifting, etc.
3. Post cast/crew check-in sheets.
4. Check attendance at call times, and make phone calls as needed.
5. Maintain order, decorum, and quiet backstage.
6. Give and/or take notes for crew heads.
7. Time (with a stop watch) each scene, shift, act, intermission, and show.

At Final Dress Rehearsal & Performances (add to previous list)

8. Arrive at least an hour and a half before curtain time.
9. Turn on work lights, shop lights, etc.
10. Unlock stage door and dressing rooms.
11. Prepare the stage so that house can be opened thirty minutes before curtain.
12. Check all stations on intercom and call system.
13. Call one hour, half-hour, fifteen minutes, places.
14. Start the show promptly.
15. Coordinate intermissions with house manager.
16. Coordinate seating interval for late arrivals with house manager, light crew, sound crew, etc.
17. Keep the show in hand — no hijinks on stage, even on closing night.
18. After each final curtain, make sure stage is cleared, everything is put away, lights are out, and doors are locked.
19. Prepare a strike plan (coordinate with building crew head).
20. Post picture call.

At Strike

1. Supervise strike.
2. Collect written reports from crew heads.
3. Submit them to teacher/director, along with your own report (timing sheets, problems encountered, solutions, suggestions, etc.).

Building Crew Head

1. Read the script.
2. Confer with the director, designer, and stage manager.
3. Obtain (and maintain) groundplans and other drawings (as needed) of the set.
4. Check inventory of tools and supplies.
5. Check inventory of stock scenery.
6. Submit to teacher written requests for additional materials (include vendor's name, address, phone number, and price of each item).
7. Pull stock units from storage; repair or alter as needed.
8. Supervise crew members in all phases of construction.
9. Supervise set-up on the stage.
10. If needed, you and your crew will become the shifting crew for tech/dress rehearsals and performances.
11. Assist the stage manager in preparing the strike plan.
12. Supervise the striking of the set.
13. Keep shop, tool cage, and all working areas neat and clean.
14. Submit a written report to the stage manager, including problems, solutions, suggestions, and expenditures.

Costume Crew Head

1. Read the script.
2. Make notes on each character.
3. Prepare a costume plot showing all characters and all scenes.
4. Confer with the director on exact requirements.
5. Fill out a costume measurement card for each cast actor.
6. Pull from stock any costumes to be used as is or with alterations.
7. Prepare a list of suggested pattern numbers and fabrics — and/or purchases from secondhand stores, etc. — including cost estimates.
8. Confer with director for approval of expenditures and final decisions on patterns and fabrics.
9. Assign sewing responsibilities to crew members, cast members, or parents.
10. Use iron-on tape to identify each cast member's costumes.
11. Prepare cardboard dividers for costume racks.

12. Keep each actor's costumes behind his or her name on the rack.

13. Supervise all on-site sewing, and check progress of articles being sewn at home.

14. Arrange fittings for actors (coordinate with stage manager).

15. Make sure all costumes are kept clean, pressed, and repaired as needed.

16. Keep all wardrobe areas clean and neat at all times.

At Dress Rehearsals and Performances

1. Caution cast members to bathe and wear deodorant, to apply makeup before costumes are put on (or with smocks to cover costumes), and *not* to smoke or eat or drink while wearing costumes.

2. Assign crew members to help with changes.

3. At dress rehearsal, sit with the director to check all costumes from the house.

4. Check each cast member before cach entrance. Have brush, safety pins, straight pins, needle and thread handy.

At Strike, and After

1. Return all accessories (shoes, hats, etc.) to storage.

2. Make sure cast members take their own clothes home, and take their costumes to be washed or cleaned.

3. Make sure all costumes are returned within one week. Check them in personally to make sure they are clean.

4. Borrowed costume pieces must be returned clean, accompanied by a thank-you note.

5. Rental costumes must be returned promptly to avoid extra costs.

6. Submit a written report to the stage manager including problems, solutions, suggestions, and expenditures.

House Manager

The House Manager is responsible for every aspect of the performance that deals directly with the audience: parking lot, sidewalks and grounds, seating area, and (sometimes) the green room.

1. Assign crew members to specific jobs and/or performances.

2. Instruct them in their duties and supervise them during each performance.

3. Attend the final dress rehearsal with your entire crew because this will be their last chance to see the entire show without interruption.

4. Arrive at the theatre at least one hour before curtain.

5. Make sure house and green room are clean and vacuumed.

6. Make sure all seats are in the "up" position, and check that all house lights and aisle lights are working.

7. Make sure the sidewalks and approaches to the theatre are clean and litter-free.

8. Be prepared to assist patrons in the parking lot (finding spaces, giving directions to the box office, etc.).

9. Make sure audience bathrooms are unlocked and clean.

10. Open the box office forty-five minutes before curtain.

11. Check with the stage manager, then open the house one-half hour before curtain.

12. Be prepared to start the show on time.

13. Coordinate seating interval for late arrivals with the stage manager.

14. Keep the box office open at least one-half hour after the show begins.

15. Inform late arrivals of the time remaining before the seating interval.

16. Make sure theatre doors are closed (and houselights are not on over-ride) when the performance is about to begin.

17. Open doors at intermission and after the show.

18. Time intermissions; call the audience back two minutes before curtain.

19. Inform the stage manager when the audience is in.

20. After each performance, pick up trash such as discarded programs from the house and green room.

21. Turn in all unused tickets, ticket stubs, and cash as soon as box office closes each performance.

22. Keep box office clean and neat.

23. Be courteous and helpful.

24. Keep doorways free of congestion.

25. Submit a written report to the stage manager after the show has closed. Include a complete account of tickets sold and cash received for each performance, total attendance for each performance, problems, solutions, and suggestions.

Light Crew Head

1. Read the script.

2. Confer with director and lighting designer about the light plot and instrument schedule.

3. Mark light cues and warns in your script.

4. Hang, plug, focus, and gel all instruments.

5. Attend rehearsals *before* first tech to get a feel for the show.

6. Coordinate your crew calls with the stage manager.

7. Working with the director and designer, set light levels for each scene.

8. Prepare detailed cue sheets.

9. Keep the control booth and instrument storage areas clean and neat.

10. Check inventory of instruments and supplies.

11. Submit written request for additional supplies, including vendor's name, address and telephone number, and price of each item.

AT TECH AND DRESS REHEARSALS

1. Arrive at least one hour before curtain.

2. Check all instruments and dimmers. Relamp, repair, or report to stage manager any malfunctions.

3. Make sure work lights are off, preshow lights are on, and house lights are at the correct level before the house is opened (one-half hour before curtain).

4. Keep in *constant* communication with the stage manager via headsets.

AT STRIKE

1. Strike all instruments (except basic set-up), gel frames, reusable gels, etc. to appropriate storage area.

2. Clear the patch panel, except for basic set-up.

3. Submit a written report to the stage manager, including problems, solutions, suggestions, and expenses.

Makeup Crew Head

1. Read the script.

2. Make notes on each character.

3. If there are makeup changes during the show, prepare a makeup plot showing all characters and all scenes.

4. Confer with the director on exact requirements.

5. Complete a makeup analysis and design worksheet with and for each cast member.

6. Check inventory of makeup supplies.

7. Submit a list of additional supplies needed, including vendor's name, address, phone, and cost for each item.

8. Arrange practice sessions for actors and crew members as needed (coordinate with stage manager).

9. Construct beards, mustaches, etc. for those cast members who can't do it themselves.

10. Keep all makeup areas clean and neat at all times.

11. Assign a mirror to each cast member; write character name on masking tape applied to top of mirror.

AT DRESS REHEARSALS AND PERFORMANCES

1. Arrive at theatre at least ninety minutes before curtain.

2. Distribute necessary makeup and supplies at each mirror.

3. Assist cast members as needed.

4. At dress rehearsal, sit with the director to check all makeup from the house.

5. Check each cast member before each entrance. Have powder, sponges, etc. handy.

6. Put away — cleaned — all makeup supplies each rehearsal/performance as soon as they are not needed.

7. Supervise cast in clearing of makeup areas; wipe down counters and mirrors as needed.

AT STRIKE, AND AFTER

1. Return all makeup and supplies — cleaned — to storage.

2. Submit a written report to the stage manager, including problems, solutions, suggestions, and expenditures.

Paint Crew Head

1. Read the script.

2. Confer with designers and director about color schemes and general effect. Help select specific painting techniques to be used.

3. Check inventory of paints, pigments, glue, brushes, and other painting equipment and supplies.

4. Submit written request for additional materials, including vendor's name, address and telephone number, and price of each item.

5. With your crew, practice all painting techniques required for the show.

6. Supervise application of all sizing, paint, and dutchman.

7. Keep all paint areas clean and neat.

8. At strike, see that all scenery painted with scene paint is washed clean and returned to stock.

9. Submit a written report to the stage manager, including problems, solutions, suggestions, and expenses.

Prop Crew Head

1. Read the script.
2. Prepare a complete list of props as called for in the script.
3. Confer with the director to discover additional props needed, or listed props that will not be needed.
4. Check inventory of props; remove to "Current Show Props" storage area anything that is appropriate either as a substitute prop or as a show prop.
5. Post in the green room a list of props we need to borrow.
6. Prepare a list of props we need to buy. Include the location and price of each item.
7. Prepare a list of props to be made in our shop. Assign crew members to make them, instructing and supervising them as they work.
8. Prepare detailed property plots for each scene; give the stage manager a copy.
9. *Before* the cast is off book, begin supplying them with show or substitute props.
10. Begin attending all rehearsals.
11. Set up props for each scene; give hand props to actors as they enter, take hand props from actors as they exit; put away all props after each rehearsal.
12. Working with the stage manager, prepare shifting schedules as necessary.
13. Keep accurate records of borrowed props; make sure they are not damaged or lost.
14. Assign specific duties to your crew for running the show.
15. Instruct and/or rehearse your crew in shifting and running techniques. Be sure they dress in dark clothing and wear soft-soled shoes.

AT TECH AND DRESS REHEARSALS AND PERFORMANCES

1. Arrive at least one hour before curtain.
2. Set the stage for the first scene. Be ready one-half hour before curtain.
3. Clean and store all props after each performance.
4. Maintain silence and darkness backstage.

AT STRIKE, AND AFTER

1. Return our props — cleaned — to permanent storage.

2. Return borrowed props, cleaned and accompanied by a written thank-you note.

3. Submit a written report to the stage manager, including problems, solutions, suggestions, and expenses.

Sound Crew Head

1. Read the script.

2. Mark sound cues and warns in your script.

3. Confer with the director about additional (or unneeded) sound cues.

4. Prepare a sound plot for the show, including for each sound: the source (tape player, CD player, etc.) and speaker for recorded sounds, and location and equipment needed for live sounds.

5. Check inventory for supplies, materials, equipment and available sounds.

6. Submit a written request for additional materials, including vendor's name, address and telephone, and exact price for each item.

7. Working with the stage manager, schedule recording dates for cast members if needed.

8. Record all effects and music (except live).

9. Be sure that all equipment and supplies are handled correctly to minimize the risk of damage. Keep control booth and work areas clean and neat.

10. Depending on available equipment, edit the sounds into a master tape to be used during the show.

11. Attend rehearsals *before* first tech to get a feel for the show.

12. Working with the director, set volume levels for all sounds.

13. Begin integrating sounds into the show two rehearsals before first tech.

At Tech and Dress Rehearsals and Performances

1. Arrive at least one hour before curtain.

2. Check all equipment and tapes; repair, resplice, and report to stage manager all malfunctions.

3. Be ready to open the house one-half hour before curtain (preshow music playing).

4. Keep in *constant* communication with the stage manager via headsets.

5. Be calm and as quiet as possible in the control booth.

At Strike

1. Store all equipment.

2. Dispose of edited tapes.

3. Prepare borrowed items for return to their owners, with written thank-you notes.

4. Submit a written report to the stage manager, including problems, solutions, suggestions, and expenses.

Running the Box Office

1. Open the box office forty-five minutes before curtain.

2. Keep tickets and money out of easy reach from the ticket window.

3. Answer the phone, " *(show title)*, may I help you?"

4. Be polite and helpful at all times. The customer is always right!

5. Be familiar with the comp list (complimentary tickets), and keep accurate records of comps distributed.

6. Be able to quote multiple ticket prices.

7. Handle each transaction this way:

    A. Take the money offered and place it on the counter.

    B. Count out the correct number of tickets and give them to the customer.

    C. Make change quickly and accurately, counting it into the customer's hand.

    D. Place the offered money into the cash box.

    E. Say, "Thank you! Enjoy the show!"

8. *Never* leave box office unattended.

9. Allow only house manager, teacher, or your relief into the box office.

10. *No* refunds or exchanges after the curtain goes up.

11. When the box office closes, make sure to have the house manager or teacher count the money and tickets and stubs *with* you.

12. You are an important contact with the public. Wear nice clothes (no tee shirts, muscle shirts, tank tops, tube tops, etc.), and *smile*!

Company Rules — Cast

1. The stage manager will issue a script to you. You are expected to bring the script to every rehearsal. You may write in the script *in pencil only.* After the show closes, you must erase your markings and return the script.

2. You will be given a list of important phone numbers (theatre, director, stage manager, etc.) to keep with your script.

3. You will also be given a rehearsal schedule. Study it to determine when you will be needed. If you anticipate any scheduling difficulties, consult with the stage manager.

4. You must report promptly for all rehearsals or other special calls. If you are ill or otherwise unavoidably detained, call the director, stage manager, or the theatre office and leave a message. Your attendance is vital. *Do not* schedule dental or medical appointments during rehearsals. If you have a job, speak with your boss *early* to arrange for time off.

5. Bring a pencil (with eraser!) to all rehearsals.

6. You are responsible for making your entrances on time. The stage manager will assist you when possible, so if you leave the immediate area of the rehearsal, make sure the stage manager knows where to find you.

7. Be respectful of your craft as an actor, of the script, the stage manager, your fellow cast members, crew members, the director/teacher, the theatre, and its equipment and supplies.

8. Advise your parents and friends that picture taking is not permitted during performances.

9. Don't tempt fate. Leave valuables and cash at home instead of in the dressing room.

10. During performances, try to avoid all contact with the audience until the show is over. Don't invite your friends backstage before the show or during intermission. Stay out of the box office, and don't peek at the audience.

11. If there is anything on the set that you need to check before curtain time, do it before the house is opened.

12. If necessary, practice applying your makeup *before* dress rehearsal.

13. Keep quiet backstage! Do not go behind the set until just before your entrance. If you must talk above the level of a whisper, you may talk in normal (not loud) tones in the dressing rooms — but don't miss your entrance!

14. Keep dressing rooms neat and clean.

15. Help crew members at strike.

16. After the show closes, take all your costumes (except for rentals) home to be washed and ironed (or dry cleaned); return them to the costume crew head within one week.

Company Rules — Crew Members

1. You will be given a list of important phone numbers (crew head, stage manager, teacher, theatre office). Commit them to memory or keep the list with you at all times.

2. If you are issued a script, remember that it remains the property of the theatre. Any marks in it should be made *in pencil only*, so they can be erased before the script is returned after the show closes.

3. You must appear promptly at all crew calls. If you are unavoidably detained or cannot attend at all, please let your crew head or the stage manager know as soon as possible. Your attendance is vital. *Do not* schedule visits to the doctor or dentist that will conflict with your crew responsibilities. If you have a job, speak with your boss *early* to arrange for time off.

4. If you have problems with your work, or your fellow crew members, or cast members, report them to your crew head. If your problem is with your crew head, talk to the stage manager. If you feel you must go even higher, speak to the director or teacher, but only as a last resort!

5. Keep your work areas and equipment clean and neat at all times.

6. Follow the directions of your crew head, stage manager, director and teacher.

7. Be respectful of our common undertaking, of your fellow students and coworkers, of the director, the teacher, your own craft and artistry in your job, the theatre building and its equipment and surroundings, and the exciting tradition of live theatre of which you are an important part.

THESE RULES APPLY PRIMARILY TO RUNNING CREWS:

8. Wear appropriate clothing. Prop and shifting crews should wear dark clothing and soft-soled shoes to tech and dress rehearsals and performances. Crew members who will be seen by the audience (ushers, house manager, light and sound crews, etc.) should wear nice clothes — no cut-offs, shorts, tank tops, tube tops, tee shirts, muscle shirts, etc. Check with your crew head if you have questions.

9. Keep quiet backstage. Stay out of the way until you are needed. If audience contact is not part of your job, avoid it like the plague. Don't invite your friends or family backstage or into the booth to keep you company before or during any rehearsal or performance.

10. Advise your family and friends that picture-taking during performances is not allowed.

Index

213

About the Author

Robert L. Lee has taught theatre arts at the high school level for over twenty-five years. He has served as the Arizona State Director, International Thespian Society. His experience includes working as an actor, designer, technician, director, and teacher in children's, high school, college, community, and professional theatre. He is a member of the Screen Actors' Guild who has appeared in many episodes of series television, as well as television movies and the theatrical film, "Terminal Velocity." In his spare time, Lee works as a graphic artist and free-lance writer. Recently, his work as an unofficial computer consultant has expanded into the world of the Internet, becoming a designer of sites for the World Wide Web.

Lee was born in Texarkana, Arkansas, in 1945, the son of public school educators, and spent his boyhood in Fort Smith, Arkansas. "Maybe my penchant for telling stories and explaining things by analogy comes from the Southern oral tradition," he speculates. He earned a B.F.A. and an M.A. in Theater Arts from the University of Arizona. He currently lives in Tucson with his wife, a daughter in high school, and a son in college. His older son lives and works in Tucson, too.

"I love the theatre," he says, "but more than that I love teaching. Students need to know that they can and should be responsible for a great deal of their own success as learners. That's partly why I wrote this book — to encourage students to become better readers and 'studiers,' skills which will stand them in good stead for the rest of their lives, even if they never take another drama course."